At Issue

What Are the Causes of Prostitution?

Other Books in the At Issue series:

At Issue

What Are the Causes of Prostitution?

Louise I. Gerdes, Book Editor

GREENHAVEN PRESS

An imprint of Thomson Gale, a part of The Thomson Corporation

THOMSON

™

GALE

Detroit • New York • San Francisco • New Haven, Conn. • Waterville, Maine • London

Christine Nasso, *Publisher*
Elizabeth Des Chenes, *Managing Editor*

© 2007 Thomson Gale, a part of The Thomson Corporation.

Thomson and Star logo are trademarks and Gale and Greenhaven Press are registered trademarks used herein under license.

For more information, contact:
Greenhaven Press
27500 Drake Rd.
Farmington Hills, MI 48331-3535
Or you can visit our Internet site at http://www.gale.com

LIBRARY OF CONGRESS CATALOGING-IN-PUBLICATION DATA

What are the causes of prostitution? / Louise I. Gerdes, book editor.
   p. cm. -- (At issue)
Includes bibliographical references and index.
ISBN-13: 978-0-7377-2737-1 (hardcover)
ISBN-10: 0-7377-2737-3 (hardcover)
ISBN-13: 978-0-7377-2738-8 (paperback)
ISBN-10: 0-7377-2738-1 (paperback)
 1. Prostitution--Juvenile literature. I. Gerdes, Louise I., 1953-
HQ118.W45 2007
306.74--dc22

                                                            2006038190

Printed in the United States of America
10 9 8 7 6 5 4 3 2 1

Contents

Introduction

During the Victorian era, society viewed prostitutes as sinful and the practice of paying for sexual services as a vice. During the mid-nineteenth century, however, society began to see prostitution as a serious social problem. Nineteenth-century research conducted by Dr. William Sanger revealed that a majority of prostitutes were poor, illiterate, and from broken families. Many turned to prostitution to survive. Nineteenth-century policymakers and activists hoping to address the problem fell into two main camps: those whose goal was to abolish prostitution and those whose goal was to regulate the practice. While the policies advocated by modern abolitionists and regulationists remain the same, their reasoning has changed dramatically.

Nineteenth-century abolitionists were Christian reformers who believed that prostitution was the ultimate social evil and should be wiped out. If a prostitute repented her evil ways and turned towards God, the abolitionists offered her shelter. If not, she would be scorned and left alone. The primary criticism of this abolitionist view was that it offered prostitutes no other way to survive, and many were forced to return to prostitution. The regulationists, on the other hand, sought to manage prostitution by legalizing it. The goal of these reformers was not to promote morality, but to control sexually transmitted diseases and crime. Unfortunately, these reformers did little to reduce either.

Modern-day abolitionists and regulationists have renewed the debate as a result of the worldwide growth in sex trafficking—the purchase, sale, recruitment, harboring, transportation, transfer, or receipt of a person for the purpose of commercial sex. Today, however, writes Amy Otchet of the United Nations Education, Scientific, and Cultural Organization, "the question is no longer about morality—is prostitution a vice and are those involved evil or somehow lacking in judgment? We now ask: is prostitution a form of exploitation to be abolished or an occupation to be regulated?"

Today's abolitionists believe that all prostitution is a form of slavery. Feminist activist Janice G. Raymond, coexecutive director of the Coalition Against Trafficking in Women, asserts that prostitution, like sex trafficking, is a human rights violation. "Prostitution," Raymond argues, "is not 'sex work,' it is violence against women. It exists because significant numbers of men are given social, moral and legal permission to buy women on demand. It exists because pimps and traffickers prey on women's poverty and inequality. It exists because it is a last ditch survival strategy, not a choice, for millions of the world's women." Because these activists believe that prostitution and sex trafficking are indistinguishable, they promote policies that oppose prostitution in all its forms.

Modern abolitionists also argue that attempts to distinguish coerced from voluntary prostitution inhibit sex-trafficking prevention efforts. According to Wendy Wright of Concerned Women of America, "If the illegality of an action swings on whether the person was willing or manipulated, there will be an enticement to create the perception that the victim volunteered." Sex traffickers, she maintains, will therefore coerce victims to tell authorities that they prostitute themselves voluntarily, using the same techniques that they use to ensnare and enslave sex-trafficking victims: assaulting and threatening the victim and family members, inducing drug dependency, confiscating passports and visas, and threatening immigrant victims with incarceration or deportation. To end sex trafficking, abolitionists assert, all prostitutes should be considered victims.

Critics of sweeping abolitionist policies that include even those who choose sex work contend that these policies do not help prostitutes but further threaten their lives and livelihood. "The moral imperative to rescue women from brothels is compelling when young girls are involved or there is clear evidence of duress," claims Susan A. Cohen, writing for the Alan Guttmacher Institute, "but 'rescuing' adult women from brothels against their will can mean an end to their health care and economic survival. In countries and situations in which basic survival is a daily struggle, the distinction between free agency and oppression may be more a gray area than a bright line." Writer Lisa Katayama agrees. "Nobody denies that trafficking is an important issue," she contends. "Nevertheless," Katayama claims, "the issue is not always as simple as it appears, and all too often crackdowns on trafficking end up cracking down on—and hurting—women who are simply trying to make a living in the sex industry, insisting on the right to ply their trade." Thus, she reasons, one-dimensional laws "are too simplistic, and often do as much harm as good."

Modern regulationists assert that national and international laws that protect workers from exploitation and other abuses can be used to protect prostitutes. Jo Bindman of Anti-Slavery International maintains, "By looking at commercial sex as work, and at the conditions under which that work is performed, sex workers can be included and protected under the existing instruments which aim to protect all workers in a general way." Viewing prostitution as a human rights violation does not erase the stigma of prostitution, regulationists claim; well-intentioned attempts to make criminals of pimps and brothel owners, rather than prostitutes, only exacerbate the problem. Laws that label pimps and brothel owners as criminals underscore the difference between prostitutes and other workers. Indeed, argues Bindman, it "reinforces the marginal, and therefore vulnerable, position of the women and men involved in prostitution."

Activists and policymakers continue to debate whether identifying prostitution as sex work will improve the well-being of prostitutes or contribute to the institutionalized abuse of women. The authors in *At Issue: What Are the Causes of*

Prostitution? debate this and other issues concerning the causes of prostitution and sex trafficking in order to determine which policies will best serve humanity.

1

The Causes of Prostitution: An Overview

Lisa A. Kramer and Ellen C. Berg

Lisa A. Kramer is working toward the completion of a Ph.D. in sociology from Arizona State University. Ellen C. Berg is currently an assistant professor of sociology at California State University, Sacramento.

The risk factors that lead women to prostitution are complex and often interrelated. Research shows, for example, that women in prostitution have high rates of childhood sexual abuse. However, less clear is whether the abuse itself leads women to prostitution or the dangerous behaviors that result from sexual abuse such as substance abuse. Studies also reveal racial differences. White prostitutes are more likely to have experienced sexual and physical abuse by a family member. Minority women, however, often enter prostitution because they have fewer economic opportunities.

Previous research has had limited success in delineating the relationships between various risk factors that appear to influence women's entry into prostitution. In addition to the problem of overcoming barriers to obtaining "meaningful information from representative samples of prostitutes," a myriad of other methodological issues arise. Risk factors most commonly associated with entry into prostitution—childhood abuse, runaway behavior, homelessness, and drug addiction—

Lisa A. Kramer and Ellen C. Berg, "Survival Analysis of Timing of Entry into Prostitution," *Sociological Inquiry*, vol. 73, November 2003, pp. 511–28. © 2003 Alpha Kappa Delta. Copyright © 2003 Basil Blackwell Ltd. Reproduced by permission of Blackwell Publishers.

are highly correlated with one another, and it is difficult to sort out their respective influences on the individual. Further, the question of causality is complex. Just as childhood abuse and drug use, for example, can increase the likelihood of entering prostitution, entry into prostitution can occur first and can increase the likelihood of experiencing various forms of physical and sexual violence. Likewise, prostitution can facilitate initial substance abuse or exacerbate existing drug use.

Women who have suffered multiple abuses within the home and elsewhere often commit and are incarcerated for the commission of survival crimes such as prostitution. The failures of specific social institutions, such as the family and the educational system, are implicated in the decision to enter prostitution, as women who are dislocated from their families and from the schools—especially women of color—are often consigned to lives of limited opportunity typified by desperate struggles for economic survival.

Childhood Sexual Abuse

Childhood sexual abuse is associated with greater vulnerability to revictimization in adulthood, including involvement in sex work. It has been well documented that women in prostitution have high rates of sexual abuse. Sexual abuse in childhood can alter an individual's orientation to the world and can distort their self-concept and emotional capacities. Sexual abuse has been shown to result in poor self-esteem, anxiety, depression, substance abuse, runaway behavior, difficulty in interpersonal relationships, and a wide array of other emotional and physical problems. Sexual-abuse victims can develop misconceptions about sex, and often display sexual knowledge and behaviors inappropriate for their age. Victims of sexual abuse have been shown to be particularly vulnerable to becoming involved in abusive and sexually exploitative relationships as adults.

In a sample of forty adolescent runaways and ninety-five homeless women, Ronald Simons and Les Whitbeck (1991) examined sexual abuse as a precursor to prostitution while controlling for variables such as parental physical abuse, substance abuse, and participation in deviant activities other than prostitution. Physical abuse was included in an effort to assess whether it is sexual abuse specifically or destructive parenting in general that is important in the etiology of prostitution. Their analyses revealed that for runaways, sexual abuse had a significant impact on the probability of entry into prostitution. Each unit increase on a sexual-abuse scale multiplied the odds of engaging in prostitution by 1.23. Simons and Whitbeck's findings are in alignment with other research suggesting that the link between previous victimization and prostitution is not direct, but rather occurs indirectly through involvement in a more dangerous lifestyle and riskier activities.

Kimberly Tyler, Dan Hoyt, and Les Whitbeck (2000) also investigated the effects of sexual abuse on subsequent sexual victimization among female homeless and runaway adolescents. Results from their analyses suggest that sexual abuse in the home has a direct positive effect on sexual victimization of adolescents on the streets. While they distinguished between sex trading and sexual victimization (positively correlated), their findings suggest an increased probability of both experiences following the development of emotional and psychological problems associated with abuse, dysfunctional family dynamics, and immersion in street culture.

Conflicting Studies

In a comparison of 237 female prostitutes and 407 women not involved in prostitution, John Potterat and colleagues (1998) examined sexual- and drug-abuse milestones in an effort to delineate pathways to prostitution. Their study showed a smaller percentage of prostitutes to have experienced sexual abuse than other studies had shown (32 percent), but this was very likely due to the fact that "nonconsensual, prepubertal sex" was defined as "penile penetration prior to age eleven." The percentage of prostitutes reporting early nonconsensual sex was still relatively high when compared to the percentage of women not involved in prostitution (13 percent). Findings from Potterat and colleagues' study support research that questions the role of sexual abuse as a direct causal variable in entering the sex trade.

In a recent investigation, Catalina Arata (2000) tested a model for predicting adult/adolescent sexual revictimization and postassault functioning for women with histories of child sexual abuse. Participants completed questionnaires regarding their sexual-victimization history, postsexual-assault symptoms and attributions, and consensual sexual behavior. Repeat victimization was defined as having experienced child sexual abuse with a separate incident of adolescent or adult victimization. Repeat victimization was positively associated with having experienced child sexual abuse. Women with repeated victimization also reported more high-risk sexual behavior.

Childhood Physical Abuse

Adult women in prostitution often report a history of childhood physical abuse as well as sexual abuse, especially at the hands of substance-abusing caregivers. In recent studies, 60–70 percent of prostitutes report being physically abused as children. While physical abuse is perhaps less frequently viewed as a precursor to entry into prostitution, long-term outcomes of physical abuse are not entirely distinct from those of sexual abuse. Similar to findings concerning sexual abuse in childhood and subsequent substance abuse, research supports that emotional problems stemming from the trauma of physical abuse in childhood can result in dependence on drugs and alcohol. In both physical and sexual abuse, the victim's body space is invaded against her wishes, often repeatedly and over an extended period of time. Additionally, physical abusers, as with sexual offenders, are often people upon whom the victim relies for care. Outcomes of physical abuse include fear, anxiety, depression, self-destructive behavior, anger, aggression, guilt and shame, an impaired ability to trust, an increased likelihood of revictimization in adulthood, sexually inappropriate behavior, school problems, truancy, running away, and delinquency.

Findings suggest that there are racial differences in the timing but not the order of the events leading to entry into prostitution.

In a recent investigation seeking to explore the extent to which child abuse is related to the persistence of risky behavior, data were collected from ninety-nine women with diagnoses of serious mental illnesses. Data pertaining to childhood sexual abuse, adult victimization, substance abuse, and risky sexual behavior were examined. Results indicated that childhood sexual abuse is related to adult sexual and physical assault, alcohol and cocaine abuse, and prostitution, but childhood physical abuse was determined to be related only to adult physical assault and alcohol abuse.

Substance Abuse by Caregivers

Children with drug-addicted parents are at extremely high risk for maltreatment. Short-term effects of parental substance abuse for children include physical health problems, hyperactivity, conduct disorders, low academic performance, learning disorders, guilt, shame, embarrassment, aggression, inability to trust others, and low self-esteem. It has been documented children of substance-abusing parents are more likely to witness domestic violence and to be victims of physical or sexual abuse. While it has been well established that the family backgrounds of prostitutes are often chaotic and dysfunctional, little research has focused specifically upon destructive parenting in the form of parental substance abuse, although one study found that 35–58 percent of prostitutes had caregivers who abused alcohol. Work by Lisa Kramer shows similar findings. Of the eighty-seven prostitutes (streetwalkers and escorts) Kramer surveyed, 67 percent grew up in homes in which one or more parents were abusing drugs and/or alcohol. In addition, for these fifty-eight households, survey respondents reported having been given illegal drugs 5 percent of the time, being given alcohol 23 percent of the time, and being given both substances 16 percent of the time prior to age eleven by a primary caregiver. While research has not specifically focused upon parental substance abuse as a precursor to entry into prostitution, given the substantive body of literature that supports dysfunctional and abusive caregivers as increasing women's risk, this appears to be a legitimate variable for further exploration.

Minority Status

Race and class oppression and the attendant poverty and homelessness increase the likelihood of minority women adopting survival strategies that involve deviant and criminal behavior. Despite the fact that minority women have been shown to suffer substantial social, educational, and economic disadvantages, studies that consider the effects of race in combination with social factors such as sexual and physical abuse are conducted relatively infrequently. Many studies have focused on the intersection of social variables such as class and gender or race and gender, but few have considered all three in conjunction. Other variables are often submerged when ethnicity or culture is examined, and very little research has explored the relationship between race and entry into prostitution specifically.

Potterat and colleagues (1998) are among the few to have substantiated racial differences among sex workers. They found that nonstreet prostitutes were more likely to be white (92 percent) than were street prostitutes (59 percent). Nonminority prostitutes were more likely than either black or Hispanic prostitutes to report IV drug use and to have experienced nonconsensual prepubertal sex. Other racial differences include significant differences between age distribution at first penile penetration, regular sexual activity, first drug use, and regular drug use. The three groups that were examined also differed significantly in the distribution of age differences between the time of first and regular prostitution. Potterat and colleagues' findings suggest that there are racial differences in the timing but not the order of the events leading to entry into prostitution. Rebecca Katz (2000) emphasizes the importance of examining women's developmental pathways to crime in ways that include an analysis of "the context of females' lives as they differ by race and class memberhip, adult and child maltreatment experiences."

White women who engaged in prostitution were more likely than minority women to have experienced sexual and physical abuse.

Studying the Causes of Prostitution

Because nonactivist prostitutes are reluctant to share information about their experiences, for legal and other compelling reasons, obtaining data from sex workers is challenging. Caution must be exercised in interpreting findings generated from any sample of subjects whose inclusion in a study is related to the ability of the researcher to gain access to them, and research with those engaging in prostitution poses no exception. As is usually the case with prostitution research, the women completing surveys for this study are, to some extent, included because they were more accessible than other women engaging in prostitution. Importantly, because street-level prostitutes are far more visible than other types of sex workers, they are arrested much more often. Thus, it is likely that the substantial majority of respondents included in this study were individuals working at the lower echelons of the prostitution hierarchy (at the street level), rather than in escort services, resorts, and/or massage parlors.

Respondents were contacted at two separate sites, resulting in a 95-percent response rate and 394 completed surveys. One group consisted of 298 women incarcerated for minor offenses (including drug offenses and solicitation of prostitution) who were participating in a voluntary program for prostitutes at the jail at the time they completed the surveys. The number of times the participants attended the weekly prostitution program ranged from one to seventeen times; according to records maintained by the program administrator, the average number of attendances was seven. The group meetings were fairly informal, facilitated discussion groups, and no therapist was present. The women were at various stages of the judicial process; some were awaiting sentencing, others had been convicted and were serving their sentences. Surveys were administered over an eighteen-month time frame beginning in 1997. The remaining ninety-six surveys were completed by women outside of prison who attended meetings or who received services from a community-based, nonresidential rehabilitation program. Due to missing data for some of the variables, the final effective sample size used in the analysis was 309 cases.

Examining the Results

This study provides several significant findings regarding childhood abuse experiences and educational achievement for nonminority and minority women working in street-level prostitution. In our sample, white women who engaged in prostitution were more likely than minority women to have experienced sexual and physical abuse by one or more family members. White women in our sample were also more likely to report alcohol or drug abuse on the part of one or more of their parents while they were growing up. Minority women's median age of entry into prostitution, however, is approximately 2.5 years younger than that of nonminority women. . . .

The findings can be interpreted in a variety of ways. As Gail Wyatt (1985) discusses, minorities and whites are not usually comparable in terms of their social-class backgrounds, and comparisons between the two groups can be problematic as a result. Diana Russell, Rachel Schurman, and Karen Trocki (1988) have pointed out that centuries of racism have resulted in minority individuals' underrepresentation in the middle and upper classes of American society and that "These class dissimilarities make it difficult to ascertain whether other differences found are due to social class or to ethnicity, or to some combination of both of these variables." In this study, it is possible that the earlier age of entry into prostitution for minority women reflects lesser economic opportunities and other disadvantages associated with lower socioeconomic status. The heavy representation of African American and other nonwhite women among the homeless mirrors their heavy concentration in the ranks of the extremely poor. Homelessness, while not examined specifically in this investigation, could be a variable worthy of future consideration. It is possible that social-class disadvantages are so compelling as to require the consideration of survival strategies such as prostitution at an earlier age due to a lack of financial and other resources. Furthermore, given that minorities disproportionately reside in poverty-stricken areas in which street-level prostitution occurs, exposure to and knowledge of the existence of prostitution may also influence minority women to enter prostitution sooner than white females, who reside in such areas to a lesser extent.

Childhood Risk Factors

The consistent impact of education on decreasing the hazard rate for entry into prostitution suggests that school may provide a less risky environment in which individuals can spend their time. The 12-percent decrease in the hazard rate attributed to each additional year of school is more likely to be due to the women's presence in school than to represent actual knowledge gained in an additional year of education. This suggests further support for Angela Browne and David Finkelhor's (1986) proposal that the involvement in risky activities or a dangerous lifestyle is important in determining the timing of entry into prostitution.

Another key finding is that the experience of a single childhood risk factor—whether it is sexual abuse or physical abuse by a family member or parental drug/alcohol abuse—appears to speed up entry into prostitution, relative to women who experience none of these risks. Additionally, minority women who experience one of these risks have a hazard rate for entry into prostitution that is approximately twice that of others in the sample. Further research using event-history analysis is likely to be useful in the examination of similar life pathways. The idea of a hazard rate associated with the entry into prostitution is conceptually rich and can be used with any variety of independent variables that are temporally prior to age of entry. As mentioned above, examination of contextual variables such as the labor market in an individual's neighborhood, socioeconomic status, and the existence of prostitution in an individual's neighborhood may be considerations worthy of future exploration. Such analyses could certainly lead to a deeper understanding of how race influences an individual's age of entry into prostitution, as neighborhoods are often highly segregated.

In conclusion, there is a great deal of room for further investigation of the life experiences and pathways that lead women to enter into prostitution. Event-history analysis may provide a particularly useful approach for exploring these issues, and the differential impact of risks on women of color clearly deserves further consideration.

2

Policies Favoring Legalization Encourage Prostitution and Sex Trafficking

Donna M. Hughes

Donna M. Hughes, professor of women's studies at the University of Rhode Island, is a leading international researcher on the trafficking of women and children.

The legalization of prostitution has not controlled prostitution. In fact, the demand for victims of sex trafficking increases when men can legally buy sex. Nor has legalization improved conditions for women forced into prostitution by poverty or a childhood of sexual abuse. Prostituted women do not join unions or sign up for benefits because many women are trafficked, and others view prostitution as a temporary solution. Prostitution is not work but a predatory and criminal business that depends on the abuse and exploitation of women.

Around the world today, there is a human rights crisis of sexual abuse of millions of women, children, and thousands of men in prostitution and other forms of sexual exploitation. There are regions of the world where prostitution has gone from being almost nonexistent to a hundred million dollar money-making industry.

Donna M. Hughes, Speech delivered at La Prostitution Feminine: Propuestas e Intervention (Female Prostitution: Proposals and Interventions), Kingston, RI: 2004. Reproduced by permission.

The Sex Trafficking, Prostitution Link

I am going to talk about prostitution and sex trafficking. I don't believe you can talk about one without the other. They are inextricably linked. Those who favor legalized prostitution have led a fifteen-year campaign to delink them—to convince us that trafficking has nothing to do with prostitution. That is false. As countries and activists who favor legalization have tried to separate prostitution and trafficking, most of the global attention has focused on trafficking. I am happy that the conference organizers in Santiago, [Spain], have had the courage to address prostitution. Still, we should be clear that we have to talk about both prostitution and trafficking together.

Sex trafficking is the process that delivers victims into prostitution. It includes the recruitment, harboring, movement, and methods by which victims are compelled to stay in prostitution, whether by violence, coercion, threat, debt, or cultural manipulation.

Prostitution and sex trafficking are based on a balance between the supply of available victims and the demand for victims to provide the sex acts. Victims are recruited from marginalized, poor, and vulnerable populations. These potential victims may be from the same city or country as the exploiters, or they may be trafficked from other countries or continents. They may be women and girls who are poor, uneducated, and naïve, and therefore easy to control, or they may be educated, middle-class girls who have been sexually abused until their bodily integrity and identities are destroyed and they no longer know how to resist abuse and exploitation.

A Demand for Victims

Prostitution and trafficking begin with the demand for victims to be used in prostitution. It begins when men go in search of sex that can be purchased. In countries where prostitution is illegal, it begins when pimps place orders with their criminal networks for women and children. In countries where prostitution is legal, it begins when brothels place job ads with government employment agencies. In places where buying sex acts is popular and profitable, pimps cannot recruit enough local women to fill up the brothels, so they have to bring in victims from other places.

Legalization does not reduce prostitution or trafficking; in fact, both activities increase.

Let me give you the example of the Czech Republic. Ten to fifteen years ago, prostitution was rare, certainly, there wasn't a sex industry. Now, according to a study by the Czech Ministry of Interior, there are over 860 brothels in the Czech Republic, of which 200 are in Prague. The Czech Republic is a destination country for Western European sex tourists. By one estimate, 65 percent of men who buy sex acts there are foreigners. The capital city has the reputation of being a "stag party" capital of Europe, meaning it is a favorite beer and sex party spot for men, mainly Great Britain and Germany. There are almost 200 web sites on the Internet for prostitution services in the Czech Republic, up from 45 in 1997, that enable sex tourists to book their travel and appointments to buy sex acts before they leave home. The Czech police estimate that there are 15,000 women and children in prostitution in the Czech Republic. Thousands of them stand along the roads or wait in roadhouses along the German and Austrian borders. Mafias control most of the victims. The Czech-German border has become a well-known site for child prostitution. German men, in particular, cross the border to buy children for sex acts. All this expansion of the sex industry has occurred in the last decade.

The Failure of Legalization

Over the past decade, the most popular proposed solutions to sex trafficking and "out of control" prostitution is legalization of prostitution. Prostitution has been legalized with the expectation that it would bring positive outcomes in Australia, the Netherlands, Germany, and recently, in New Zealand. Although legalization has resulted in big legal profits for a few, the other benefits have not materialized. Organized crime groups continue to traffic women and children and run illegal prostitution operations alongside the legal businesses. In Victoria, Australia, legalization of brothels was supposed to eliminate street prostitution. It did not; in fact, there are many more women on the street than before legalization. Last year, there were calls for legalizing street prostitution in order to "control it."

Legalization does not reduce prostitution or trafficking; in fact, both activities increase because men can legally buy sex acts and pimps and brothel keepers can legally sell and profit from them. Cities develop reputations as sex tourist destinations. In the Netherlands, since legalization, there has been an increase in the use of children in prostitution.

German lawmakers thought they were going to get hundreds of millions of euros in tax revenue when they legalized prostitution and brothels. But [in] keeping with [the] criminal nature of prostitution, the newly redefined "business owners" and "freelance staff" in brothels will not pay their taxes. Germany is suffering a budget deficit, and the Federal Audit Office estimates that the government has lost over two billion euros a year in unpaid tax revenue from the sex industry. Recently, lawmakers started to look for ways to increase collection of taxes from prostitutes. This has put the government into the traditional role of pimp—coercing prostitutes to give them more money.

This predatory behavior of the government sharply contrasts to the promised benefits of legalization in Germany, such as government benefits and rights for women. Legalization was supposed to enable women to get health insurance and retirement benefits, and enable them to join unions.

The normalization of prostitution as work has not occurred in Germany, the Netherlands, or Australia. Following legalization, few women have signed up for benefits or for unions. The reason has to do with the basic nature of prostitution. It is not work; it is not a job like any other. It is abuse and exploitation that women only engage in if forced to or when they have no other options. Even where prostitution is legal, a significant proportion of women is trafficked. Women and children controlled by pimps and mafias cannot register with an authority or join a union. Women who are making a more or less free choice to be in prostitution do so out of immediate necessity—debt, unemployment, and poverty. They consider resorting to prostitution as a temporary means of making money, and assume as soon as a debt is paid or a certain sum of money is earned for poverty-stricken families, they will go home. They seldom tell friends or relatives what they are doing to earn money. They do not want to register with authorities and create a permanent record of being a prostitute. And unionization of "sex workers" is a fantasy; it is completely incompatible with the coercive and abusive nature of prostitution.

Instead of legalization, there is another solution to the problem of prostitution and sex trafficking: Confronting the demand for prostitution. Instead of only warning women against recruiters, stop the recruiters. Instead of accommodating the demand, stop it.

The Abolitionist Movement

There is a growing abolitionist movement around the world that seeks to provide assistance to victims and hold perpetrators accountable.

In Sweden, beginning in 1999, the purchasing of sexual services became a crime. The new law was passed as part of a new violence-against-women act that broadened the activities that qualified as criminal acts of violence. With this new approach, prostitution is considered to be one of the most serious expressions of the oppression of and discrimination against women. The focus of the law is on "the demand" or the behavior of the purchasers of sex acts, not the women.

The U.S. government has adopted an abolitionist approach at the federal level. In 2003, U.S. president George W. Bush issued a Presidential Directive. It was the first U.S. opinion on the link between prostitution and trafficking: "Prostitution and related activities, which are inherently harmful and dehumanizing, contribute to the phenomenon of trafficking in persons. . . ." This policy statement is important because it connects trafficking to prostitution and states that prostitution is harmful. This policy goes against attempts to delink prostitution and trafficking and redefine prostitution as a form of work for women.

If there were no men seeking to buy sex acts, no women and children would be bought and sold.

In a United Nations speech in October 2003, President Bush called attention to the demand side of prostitution and trafficking. He said, "Those who patronize [the sex industry] debase themselves and deepen the misery of others. And governments that tolerate the trade are tolerating a form of slavery." This statement has led the departments of government, including the U.S. State Department to focus more attention and funding on the demand side of prostitution and sex trafficking.

The Root Cause

I believe that only by going to the root cause of prostitution and trafficking, which are the factors that make up the demand, will we end the sexual exploitation and abuse of women and children through prostitution and trafficking.

We need to urge all governments, NGOs, and religious communities to focus on reducing the demand for victims of sex trafficking and prostitution. All the components of the demand need to be penalized—the men who purchase sex acts, the exploiters—the traffickers and pimps who profit from the sale of women and children for sex, the states that fund deceptive messages and act as pimp, and the culture that lies about the nature of prostitution.

We could greatly reduce the number of victims, if the demand for them was penalized. If there were no men seeking to buy sex acts, no women and children would be bought and sold. If there were no brothels waiting for victims, no victims would be recruited. If there were no states that profited from the sex trade, there would be no regulations that facilitated the flow of women from poor towns to wealthier sex industry centers. If there were no false messages about prostitution, no women or girls would be deceived into thinking prostitution is a glamorous or legitimate job.

3

The Root Cause of Prostitution Is the Demand for Prostitutes

Lisa A. Howard

Lisa A. Howard is an American criminologist living in Stockholm, Sweden.

If there were no demand for paid sexual services, there would be no prostitution. Based on this reasoning, the Swedish government has criminalized the purchase of sexual services. By punishing the buying of sex, Sweden has reduced the demand, which has in turn reduced prostitution. As long as men believe it is their right to purchase and exploit women and children, prostitution and sex trafficking will remain a serious problem.

I have an American friend who works in an adjoining crystal shop with an exclusive hotel here in Stockholm. She was approached recently while on the job by an average-looking traveling man (staying at the hotel) who asked if she knew where he could find "women". "What?" my friend inquired. "You know, Swedish 'massage parlors', women . . . you know . . ." replied the man. "I *don't* know!" my friend heatedly responded. Is it so difficult to buy sex in Stockholm—even in the inner-city—that he had to ask in a fine crystal shop?

When I met with Gunilla Ekberg (the Special Advisor on issues of prostitution and trafficking in women at the Swedish

Lisa A. Howard, "Prostitution: 'The Oldest Profession in the World'—Is It Possible to Reduce Demand?" captive daughters.org, www.captivedaughters.org/demaddynamics/reducedemand.htm, Reproduced by permission.

Division for Gender Equality) recently I asked if the relatively 'new' tougher legislation on the buying of sexual services is 'working'—i.e., reducing demand of such services—in Sweden, she said, "Look around, did you see any women standing on the streets on your way here?" (Ms. Ekberg's office sits in one of the former most popular districts for prostitutes). And it's true, if you take a look around this capital city you will be hard-pressed to find women and girls standing on the streets and even more difficult to find brothels and the so-called 'Swedish massage parlors'. It is not some kind of illusion that Stockholm has created. The fact that a man had to ask in a fine crystal shop for "women" is proof of the success. Actually, I deliver this message to all possible solicitors of sexual services who are planning to travel to Sweden: Don't come to Sweden. You will not have success here. "It is a crime to buy sex in Sweden" as the campaign to combat prostitution and trafficking in women by the Regeringskansliet (The Office of the Government of Sweden) proclaims.

If men did not regard it as their self-evident right to purchase and sexually exploit women and children, prostitution and trafficking would not exist.

A Form of Exploitation

"In Sweden, prostitution is regarded as an aspect of male violence against women and children. It is *officially* acknowledged as a form of exploitation of women and children and constitutes a significant social problem, which is harmful not only to the individual prostituted woman or child, but also to society at large", according to the Ministry of Industry, Employment and Communications.

Therefore, in 1999, the Swedish Parliament passed "a law that only criminalized the *buying* of sexual services". Moreover, the new legislation makes it a criminal offense to purchase or even attempt to purchase sexual services and is punishable by day fines and/or imprisonment. The women and children, seen as the victims, are not criminalized and will be offered social benefits and advice in an effort to help them "break-away" from prostitution or trafficking, giving them alternatives that they previously did not have. To underline Swedish seriousness in matters of these issues a new law was passed in July 2002 "against trafficking in human beings for sexual purposes ... this means that all the links in the prostitution and women-trafficking chain have been made a criminal offense in Sweden: the buyers of women and children in prostitution, pimps and traffickers in women". It is essential to understand that "without prostitution, there would be no trafficking in women". Certainly, we can draw the conclusion that without the demand of sexual services there would be no prostitution.

The Root Cause

When considering how to reduce demand of prostitution a 'root-cause' discussion needs to be brought to the table. Ms. Ekberg states that the root cause of this demand is "men", their demand for women and children. Before putting this article down, consider that statistically speaking "prostitution is a gender-specific phenomenon; the overwhelming majority of victims are women and girls, while the perpetrators are invariably men". To respond to the age-old comment of the prolegalization movement, "It's the oldest profession in the world", take into account this point: "If men did not regard it as their self-evident right to purchase and sexually exploit women and children, prostitution and trafficking would not exist. Human traffickers and pimps profit from women's and girls' economic, social, political and legal subordination". On this note, consider that the internationally accepted median age for entrance of girls into prostitution is fourteen years of age. How many of us believe that the majority of these young girls—children—thought prostitution would be a good career move?

Reducing the Demand

Efforts can be made in reducing the oppression of women by reducing the demand of sexual services. Undeniably this is not easy to achieve in a patriarchal society. In my conversation with Gunilla Ekberg she expressed that the Swedish legislation did not occur overnight and much debate took place over a period of years where people were "questioning men's perceived unlimited sexuality with anyone for the first time". According to Ms. Ekberg there are three main recommendations that the prolegislation movement can do to reduce the demand of sexual services in the United States:

- A public debate needs to take place. Open discussions on issues such as the "sexualization" of women, the root causes of prostitution and the effects of a patriarchal society and make visible the men who procure or attempt to procure sexual services (as the typical buyer does not come from the marginalized sector of society).

- Programs for exiting from prostitution need to be developed.

- Educate the enforcers, i.e., the police and the prosecutors.As a conclusion, the first step to eradicate prostitution is to turn the tide and make it a crime *only* to buy sexual services. Quit punishing the women—the victims—and focus on the demand of such services extrapolating that the demand causes the supply. The only way the U.S. can say that it is a democracy is when all the people are equal and as long as women are bought and sold as commodities gender equality will not be achieved.

4

Poverty Leads to Prostitution in the Developing World

Carol Mithers

Carol Mithers writes articles and commentary on women's issues for publications such as O, the Oprah Magazine *and* Ladies' Home Journal.

The root cause of prostitution and sex trafficking in the developing world is poverty. Some women are tricked into prostitution with the promise of a job, and others come from desperate families that are willing to sacrifice a daughter to prostitution to feed the family The problem is exacerbated by governments that turn a blind eye to the problem and by corrupt officials who profit from brothels. To end the trafficking and prostitution of women and children, economic conditions in developing nations must improve.

Midnight—Phnom Penh, Cambodia. In the warm, humid night, men seeking sex cruise the groups of women clustered at the edges of parks in this graceful capital city. The typical encounter is brutish, raw. Under a large tree almost within view of the home of the country's prime minister, a man paws a woman's breasts and pushes her onto the grass for intercourse. He's done in minutes; then she rejoins the others. As the hours pass, the scene repeats again and again. The laughing customers probably know that most of these young women have been trafficked—forced or tricked into becoming sex workers. The men seem not to care. They don't

Carol Mithers, "Rescuing the World's Girls, Part 2: The Garden of Evil," *O, the Oprah Magazine*, vol. 5, November 2004. Reproduced by permission of the author.

want to hear stories of bitter childhood poverty, of parents so frantic to survive that they said yes to a stranger's vague promise of a big city "job" for their daughter.

Feeling the Violence

But these are the tales that obsess one woman who stands among them. Although she's considerably older than the others, in the dark she blends in, with her slender build, heavy makeup, and tight, sexy clothes. When customers appear, the young women move protectively in front of her; she is there to bear witness. Mu Sochua, fifty, began this work while serving as Cambodia's minister of women's and veterans' affairs. [In the summer of 2004] she left her post to join her country's opposition party; she continues to learn the harsh truth by walking with those who walk the streets. "I am very frightened on these nights. But I want to feel the violence, the abuse, the reality of these women," she says quietly, with controlled passion. Her gestures are economical and contained. "There is no way I could learn about this by reading a report."

The street is where Sochua hears about police who extort bribes or rape the women they arrest; of the shanties where young men from wealthy families bond by gang-raping streetwalkers; of the methods by which poverty-stricken women and children are drawn into the sex industry. It's where she absorbs the harsh details of that life: Sex in the park is exchanged for the equivalent of one U.S. dollar, even less after 10 P.M., with as much as half given to a pimp. Sochua counts hundreds of young girls, many infected with HIV, some the same age—thirteen—as her youngest daughter. "I am always holding back tears," Sochua says. "With all the power I have, how can I not stop this?"

More than two decades ago, Sochua finished graduate school in the United States. She could have stayed to enjoy a relatively comfortable career in social work. Instead she returned to her homeland to become a passionate fighter for girls and women. Her drive to transform a society shattered by war into one that's fair and equal has led her to tackle one of the worst human rights problems of our time.

Children are often sold by parents desperate enough to sacrifice one daughter to feed the rest of the family.

A Global Outrage

Sex trafficking is a global outrage that victimizes millions: Nepalese women are sold into India; sub-Saharan Africans into Belgium; Nigerians into Italy, Germany, and France; Filipinas throughout much of the world, including North America; and those from the former Soviet bloc all throughout Europe. In 2000 the United States passed the Victims of Trafficking and Violence Protection Act, which calls for a yearly evaluation of more than 100 countries. In 2003 it became much easier to prosecute U.S. citizens traveling abroad for the purpose of having sex with children. Yet roughly 10,000 girls and young women, mostly from East Asia and the Pacific, are in the United States, working in strip clubs, massage parlors, and brothels.

Cambodia is one of the most active trafficking centers in the world. In theory prostitution is illegal, but in practice a majority of Cambodian men regularly buy sex. The country, with a population of 13 million, has as many as 80,000 sex workers, a huge number of whom are under sixteen. And children as young as five are smuggled from Vietnam into Cambodia, where, in a village just outside Phnom Penh, they service a local and international clientele of pedophiles. In 2002 *Time* magazine reported a description of Cambodia as a "pervert's paradise."

Trafficking here works the way it does everywhere else: Some women are abducted, others tricked with the promise of a job or told they've been sold and have to work off the "debt."

Children are often sold by parents desperate enough to sacrifice one daughter to feed the rest of the family. Many of these girls are imprisoned, beaten, and forced to service dozens of men daily. If they're taken to foreign countries and escape, they may be jailed as illegal immigrants. And girls who manage to make it home are often rejected by their families.

The most depressing aspect of trafficking is its persistence, but Sochua is a formidable warrior in the fight against it. "She has an extraordinary ability to go to the root of the problem," says Kavita Ramdas, president and CEO of the San Francisco-based Global Fund for Women, which has funded several of her efforts. At that root lie poverty and lack of education. "Sochua has a quality of gentleness, which masks a steeliness below. Once she decides to do something, you can't stop her. Zen Buddhists would say she's like water—it may flow very gently but can wear down the hardest stone."

Women Are Precious Gems

In 1991, shortly after Sochua's third daughter, Malika, was born, she began a women's organization that put together credit programs, shelters for victims of domestic violence, and demonstrations for peace held in cooperation with local Buddhist monks and nuns. Seven years later, she successfully ran as a national assembly candidate, and soon afterward she was asked to take over the Ministry of Women's and Veterans' Affairs, which had always been run by a man. Her first act was to begin a national campaign to rewrite an old Cambodian proverb: "It says, 'A man is gold; a woman is a white piece of cloth,'" Sochua says. "Think of it. If you drop a piece of gold in the mud, you can clean it, and it will be shinier than before. But if a piece of white cloth is stained, it is ruined. If you've lost your virginity, if you're a battered woman, you cannot be a white piece of cloth. Within a week, someone on my staff came up with 'Men are gold. Women are precious gems.'"

The now widely recognized image of women as gems is central to Sochua's antitrafficking efforts. Gender inequality is nothing new in Cambodia, where traditionally girls have been far less likely than boys to be educated, and until Sochua proposed a law addressing domestic violence in 2003, there hadn't been one. (The law is, in fact, still pending.) Publicity is also crucial to Sochua's efforts, and she doesn't hesitate to go for the gut. In one of a series of video and television ads, scenes of a sobbing young girl being taken from her family to a brothel are juxtaposed with those of a squealing pig heading to slaughter. It ends with the sound of the girl's screams as she's raped by man after man and the stern admonition that "women and children are human beings, not animals."

She also takes her case directly to the people in rural villages. "You travel through rice fields, potholes, dust," she says. "Each village has maybe 100 families, and they walk to where we show a movie. I always pick out one old woman in the audience. 'Grandmother,' I'll say, 'your earrings are so beautiful! And old! Where did you get them?' She'll answer, with a big smile, 'Oooh, they come from when I was married forty years ago.'

"'What is their value?'

"'Oooh, I don't know. I'd never sell them.'

"'Why not, Grandmother? How come you've held on to those earrings through the war, through everything?'

"'Because they're so precious, Granddaughter.'

"And that's it. I've got her. Now I can say, 'What else is precious? Your children are precious. If you let your daughters go, your family heritage is gone. They are your gems. Love them. Educate them. Protect them.' Everywhere I go, women come up to me and say, 'Now I realize what you mean. Find my daughter!' When that happens, we try to get word out. Maybe 10 percent of those girls we find."

Speaking Out Against Corruption

Sochua also speaks out against official corruption—"in the ministry of commerce, the ministry of labor, the judiciary, the police. When thousands of children are in brothels practically in the middle of the city, and the foreign press writes about it, how could the prime minister not know?" The blunt truth, she says, is that while traffickers may be part of organized criminal gangs, in many places local police and village chiefs are involved, and those in power profit from it. (According to Janice Raymond, coexecutive director of the Coalition Against Trafficking in Women, sexual trafficking is worth some $10 billion a year globally. Although there are no firm figures for Cambodia, the International Labour Organization estimates that in countries like Malaysia and Thailand, the sex industry accounts for 2 to 14 percent of the gross domestic product.) Sochua has created a list of foreign pedophiles known to patronize Cambodian brothels, aimed at blocking these men from entering the country and at deporting those who are already there. One deported American, says Sochua, was running a pornographic Web site that featured hundreds of Cambodian children.

Faced with hunger, women sell their children into the sex industry.

In May [2004] Sochua helped broker a deal with Thailand allowing trafficked Cambodians to go home rather than be thrown in jail as illegal immigrants; she has crafted a similar arrangement with Vietnam. If these victories seem small, they aren't to the families involved. "Just recently, we were able to bring back seven girls," says Sochua. "Several were under sixteen. I went to the airport. I saw the mothers, the tears and pain. They grab their children. It's so difficult for me because I'm a mother, too. The guilt you see, the loss of innocence— nothing can give that back. And the story doesn't end there.

What emotional and psychological support will these girls get? None. Zero. They will have to be strong and pick up their lives. That's why we go back to 'Women are precious gems.' Even after what happened to them, those girls are still precious."

Providing Alternatives

The final piece of Sochua's strategy is to give women the financial ability to resist traffickers. "You can't end trafficking until people have another way to live," she points out. "Right now about five million men, women, and children make less than 50 cents a day—so 85 percent of our young women and girls volunteer to go out of their villages to look for work. Maybe 15 percent find jobs—where do the rest go? Faced with hunger, women sell their children into the sex industry." She refuses to judge them: "I have to say, 'Did they have a choice when they let their daughters go?' I don't think they did. We have started one great program, though it's very small, at the village level. Women borrow about $100 to buy a cart, and they sell locally made products to tourists. The message is 'Give women a chance.'" She pauses. "What makes me desperate is that I can't find enough money to help them all get started."

Sochua's willingness to point an accusatory finger at traffickers, police, and her own government carries a high price. She says that her telephone is tapped, and even on trips to the United States, she finds herself constantly looking over her shoulder. The possibility of being killed for her activism "is something I don't want to think about." Constant immersion in human misery also takes a psychic toll. "I have to block it," she says. "When it's too much, I take a shower and I run the water hard, very hot, then very cold, and then I cry and cry and cry. In public I cannot be seen in tears—the men will say, 'See, even as a minister, she cries! Women are so weak.' But if I were not to continue, I could not sleep. I don't think I could face my children."

5

Poverty Is Not Always the Cause of Prostitution in the Developing World

Bruce Bower

Bruce Bower is a staff writer for Science News, *a weekly newsmagazine covering research in all fields of science.*

The assumption that poverty is the root cause of prostitution leads to broad and simplistic solutions. The problem of prostitution among women and girls from rural northern Thailand, for example, is not a result of poverty. Indeed, it is a cultural requirement that girls earn money to improve the family's financial status. In fact, girls from both poor and relatively well-off rural Thai families become prostitutes. Therefore, education and job training programs may be ineffective to reduce prostitution in developing nations such as Thailand.

For people concerned with child welfare and human rights, the rural villages of northern Thailand loom as a heart of darkness. National policies on land ownership have led to the demise of many family farms in this agricultural area during the past thirty years, so northern Thais have increasingly trekked far from home in search of jobs. A well-publicized and shocking aspect of this phenomenon has been the massive trafficking of Thai women and girls from the north in the sex industry of Bangkok and of cities in richer Asian nations.

It's unclear precisely how many child prostitutes Thailand has produced. The U.N.'s [United Nation's] International La-

Bruce Bower, "Childhood's End: In Thailand, Poverty Isn't the Primary Reason That Girls Become Prostitutes," *Science News*, September 24, 2006. Copyright © 2005 Science Service, Inc. Reproduced by permission.

bor Organization estimates that 100,000 to 200,000 Thai women and girls work in a variety of overseas venues where sex is sold. The Protection Project, a human rights research institute in Washington, D.C., places the number of Thai females participating in Japan's commercial sex market alone at between 50,000 and 70,000.

U.N. and human rights groups alike have assumed that prostitution and other forms of child exploitation stem from a toxic social brew of poverty mixed with a lack of education and job training. Antiprostitution programs in northern Thailand—a limning region without a major city—now focus on promoting better schooling for girls and teaching vocational skills to villagers.

Challenging Conventional Wisdom

Enter Lisa Rende Taylor. An anthropologist at the Asia Foundation, a nonprofit policy-and-research organization headquartered in San Francisco, Rende Taylor directed a fourteen-month study of child labor, prostitution, and sex trafficking in two northern Thai villages. Her results, published in the June [2005] *Current Anthropology*, challenge conventional wisdom about why so many of the region's girls end up selling their bodies in brothels, massage parlors, teahouses, and snack bars across Asia.

Many northern Thai girls regard prostitution as a 'bearable choice.'

"Neither poverty nor lack of education are the driving forces behind trafficking of northern Thai children," Rende Taylor says. Daughters from both poor and relatively well-off families become prostitutes in roughly equal proportions, she finds. Moreover, some girls who complete primary or even secondary levels of education also enter the sex trade.

A Bearable Choice

Many northern Thai girls regard prostitution as a "bearable choice," according to Rende Taylor, because they feel obligated to repay their parents for past sacrifices and to improve the family's financial standing. That obligation stands even if the parents own farmland and make a decent living. In a setting devoid of any other well-paying job opportunities, the oldest profession represents the only way for a girl to make enough money to maintain or enhance her family's property and status in the village. In landowning families, middle-born daughters are the most likely to become prostitutes.

First-born girls typically stay at home to assist their parents in daily tasks and thus rarely enter the sex trade. Middle-born girls are traditionally regarded as the family's financial helpers. Thanks to the labor of their older sisters, last-born girls typically receive more schooling than their sisters. Still, it's not uncommon for them, too, to spend time as prostitutes after completing the equivalent of elementary or high school. They work to recoup education costs and strengthen family finances, Rende Taylor says.

"It's common for one female sibling to be working in the fields alongside the parents, another to be working in a bar in Bangkok, and perhaps another getting a secondary education," remarks Rende Taylor.

In contrast, parents don't expect much payback from sons, who move into the homes of their wives' families after marriage.

Female prostitution in northern Thailand is often a family choice, Rende Taylor says. Therefore, interventions to stop sex trafficking must address such factors as a girl's need to earn money for family status. Such an approach would differ from methods used elsewhere around the world, where human rights workers have good reason to suspect that many youngsters sell sex because they've been coerced, abandoned, kidnapped, or sold into virtual slavery to pay off parental debts.

Family Ties

It's daunting to ask women in a foreign country to talk about how many of their daughters work as prostitutes and why they permit them to do so. And it's especially difficult to get honest answers.

In her fieldwork, Rende Taylor had two advantages in gaining the trust of residents in a pair of northern Thai farming villages, each consisting of about 150 families. First, being half Thai herself and having relatives in a neighboring province of Thailand, she spoke the native language and looked much like the women whom she was studying. Second, her research team consisted of six women from nearby villages who were aware of how area girls were recruited to work in sex emporiums throughout Asia.

Daughters of landowning and landless parents entered the sex trade with comparable frequency.

Moreover, village headmen had approved of the study and were consulted during the project.

During parts of 1999, 2001, and 2002, Rende Taylor's team interviewed all currently or formerly married women in the two villages, a total of 299 individuals. Their ages ranged from 18 to 109. With assistance from some of the women's adult children, the researchers chronicled the personal histories of the women and their 677 children. The team noted amounts of education, jobs held, number of marriages, and long-distance moves.

Studying Prostitution in Thailand

Of 244 daughters performing full-time labor of some kind, 62 had been involved in commercial sex work. Many had recruited village girls for sex traffickers or served as prostitutes in Bangkok, Malaysia, Singapore, or Japan. The other daughters worked primarily in sweatshops or as scavengers.

Daughters of landowning and landless parents entered the sex trade with comparable frequency and almost always with their parents' knowledge. Land is the major currency of wealth in northern Thailand, as most farming families don't save any cash.

Middle-born daughters from landowning families were about twice as likely to do stints as prostitutes as their sisters were. Birth order made little difference in landless families, where prostitution surged among girls whose mothers had remarried.

Stepfathers and step siblings may have put extra pressure on girls to earn family money in the high-wage sex industry, Rende Taylor suggests.

It is important to get away from unhelpful stereotypes of passive trafficked victims.

In all families, daughters involved in prostitution remitted large amounts of money to their parents. Several families used the income to build huge, fancy houses next to the older, wooden-stilt houses of neighbors.

In an economy that offers girls no viable alternatives for earning enough money to meet family obligations, prostitution is viewed as an acceptable, if still socially frowned-upon, choice, Rende Taylor asserts.

At the same time, Buddhist beliefs in northern Thailand contribute to community acceptance of former prostitutes, who often marry local men, says Rende Taylor. Thai Buddhists hold that each person's soul inhabits many physical bodies over time, with the quality of each life influenced by the soul's store of merit. Prostitution performed out of the need to aid one's family builds up merit, despite the nature of the job itself.

Most former prostitutes that Rende Taylor's team spoke to said that they had worked short hours and had had the freedom to choose or reject clients. The women generally didn't regret what they had done.

"The trauma inflicted on a Thai woman's psyche by commercial sex work may be different from and, barring coercion or violence, less than that sustained by a Western woman," Rende Taylor suggests.

Child Support

In 1993 and 1994, anthropologist Heather Montgomery of the Open University in Milton Keynes, England, interviewed fifty Thai girls who worked as prostitutes in a slum adjacent to a tourist resort. These girls' reported feelings of indebtedness to their parents and desire to repay them financially were echoed in Rende Taylor's more-recent findings, Montgomery says.

A twelve-year-old girl, who had earned enough money from one sex client to rebuild her parents' house, excitedly told Montgomery, "I will make merit for looking after my parents." The young Buddhist believed that such merit would bless her in her next life and negate the effects of having been a prostitute.

Montgomery wrote about her experiences with such children in a 2001 book *Modern Babylon? Prostituting Children in Thailand* (Berghahn Books, Oxford).

Observations such as Montgomery's, as well as Rende Taylor's report, illuminate the reasoning of some child prostitutes. "If policy makers are serious about ending the problem . . . it is important to get away from unhelpful stereotypes of passive trafficked victims," Rende Taylor says.

In her opinion, intervention projects should open to local Thai girls key positions that are held in high esteem by villagers and typically filled by outsiders with more education than the locals have. These jobs include bookkeeping, government administration, and research for international companies targeting goods to the Thai market. Young women holding these jobs could stay in their home villages while bringing status and income to their families.

The new data raise the prospect that Thai families hedge their bets by sending only some of their daughters into prostitution. Psychologist Christine Liddell of the University of Ulster in Londonderry, Northern Ireland, says that the parents studied by Rende Taylor often selected middle-born girls for prostitution to limit any damage to household functioning should the risky venture fail to yield much revenue or result in harm to a child. For farming families facing uncertain prospects, first-born "home helpers" and well-schooled last borns may be less expendable than middle borns are, Liddell says.

She argues that increasing demands for children in the global sex trade and the continuing decline in numbers of family farms in Thailand promote child prostitution far more than any calculated decisions by northern Thai parents do.

Given the limited size of Rende Taylor's study, it's not clear that parents have much say in whether their daughters become prostitutes, remarks anthropologist Bernard Formoso of the University of Paris. Parents probably permitted girls and boys alike to seek their destinies—an important concept in Buddhism—by temporarily migrating to cities such as Bangkok, where some girls entered the sex trade, he says.

Rende Taylor disagrees. Parents are indeed urging their children into prostitution, she reports. Her findings reflect a "dangerous tradeoff" that northern Thai families make. In her view, parents permit certain daughters to face prostitution's hazards in order for the family to reap its unparalleled financial returns.

Disease Dangers

A frightening specter looms over the entire business of selling sex—the possibility of contracting and spreading AIDS and other sexually transmissible diseases.

45

Rende Taylor has yet to explore whether or how concerns about AIDS influence the decisions of northern Thai families to permit their daughters to become prostitutes. The disease has certainly made its presence known in the two villages where she worked. In 2002, 13 percent of families in one village and 3 percent of those in the other reported one or more members infected with HIV or diagnosed with AIDS.

A decade ago, Thai prostitutes who spoke to Montgomery repeatedly told her that they would get pregnant or contract diseases only if it was their fate. Thus, they almost never used contraceptives or received medical checkups.

In northern Thailand, increasing rates of HIV infection among former prostitutes may soon cause at least some parents to keep their daughters out of the sex trade, predicts anthropologist Monique Borgerhoff Mulder of the University of California, Davis.

Rende Taylor regards only one thing as certain: The phenomenon of child prostitution can look dramatically different through the eyes of those whom it directly affects.

6

Childhood Sexual Abuse Often Leads to Prostitution

Kari Lydersen

Kari Lydersen is a staff writer for the Washington Post *and teaches at the Urban Youth International Journalism Program in Chicago.*

Many women who become prostitutes have been victims of childhood sexual abuse. To cope with the trauma of sexual abuse and the stress of prostitution, many turn to drugs and alcohol, which further complicates their problems. If society is to prevent prostitution, it must condemn the sexual abuse of women and children.

Growing up on Chicago's South Side, Brenda Myers looked up to the prostitutes working outside her window. "I asked my grandmother what those women were doing. She said, 'They take their panties off for money.'"

At age nine this idea didn't strike Myers as odd—a family member had been molesting her for years—and she grew up understanding that her body would be the way she got by: "I was thinking, well, they're already taking my panties off, and I wasn't getting any money. So I'll make them pay for it," she says.

She did, and like a majority of women working the streets, Myers became mired in a cycle of dependency on drugs, alcohol, prostitution, and abusive relationships—a cycle that starts in youth and ends up landing them in jail and prison.

Women are the fastest growing segment of the incarcerated—more than 91,000 were in state and federal prisons in 2000 (a figure that does not include jails). While the number of incarcerated men grew by 77 percent between 1990 and 2000, the female population grew by 108 percent, according to U.S. Department of Justice [DOJ] statistics.

A 1995 study . . . found that people who were sexually abused as children are a whopping 27.7 times more likely than others to be arrested for prostitution.

Like Myers, about half the women behind bars are there for nonviolent offenses, primarily prostitution- and drug-related violations and petty theft or fraud, according to the DOJ.

Childhood Experiences Loom Large

And like Myers, a significantly high number of them are victims of childhood sexual abuse. A recent study by the Chicago Coalition for the Homeless reported that 41 percent of women arrested for prostitution-related offenses in Cook County jail were sexually abused as children.

The Illinois Coalition Against Sexual Assault (ICASA) conducted a study in which 57 percent of women working as prostitutes in the state reported they were sexually abused as children. The study also found that more than 90 percent lost their virginity through assault, and 70 percent believed being sexually abused as children influenced their decision to become prostitutes.

Likewise, a 1995 study by the National Criminal Justice Reference Service found that people who were sexually abused as children are a whopping 27.7 times more likely than others to be arrested for prostitution.

As Myers describes, many prostitutes say they turned to paid dates as a way to take control of their sexuality after having had it taken from them. Others are forced into prostitution by their abusers—a 2001 study by the Center for Impact Research (CIR) noted that it is common for adults in particularly dire circumstances to force children into prostitution to pay rent or to buy drugs.

A number of women interviewed in Chicago tell similar stories of how they ended up in and out of jail on drug- and prostitution-related offenses. It starts with childhood sexual abuse by a relative or mother's boyfriend, a lifelong psychological trauma for which they often never receive counseling or treatment. Growing up in households where substance abuse and prostitution are prevalent, the women started both at a young age. According to the CIR study, 62 percent of prostitutes have their first "date" before age eighteen.

"My mother's ex-husband used to have me up in the middle of the night giving him head," says Louise Lofton, another former prostitute in Chicago, who has worked with Myers to form a group called Exodus to help women leave prostitution.

"One time she came in unexpectedly, and he started beating her because he knew he was in the wrong; he wanted to cover up for himself," Lofton says. "I ran into him once when I was in prostitution—I had this leopard print skirt on. I said, 'This is because of you.' He said, 'I'm sorry.' I said, 'Fuck you.'"

Untreated Addictions

Studies also show that almost all women working in prostitution use drugs and alcohol heavily. Many start using these substances or increase their usage in order to deal with the stress and emotional issues of the trade. Others begin to prostitute themselves to fund their drug habits or those of their partners or family members.

For many, the specter of sexual abuse lies behind it all—driving them to seek solace or release in drugs and sex and complicating attempts to change their lives and recover.

"The drug abuse is just one part of it," says Tracy Banks-Geiger, the court and jail program coordinator at Genesis House, a free residential recovery program for women in prostitution in Chicago. "There are also issues of poverty, racism and childhood sexual abuse that never received any treatment."

Doing Harder Time

Women bear the brunt of prostitution incarcerations. Johns usually face heavy fines—under a Chicago city ordinance they are charged $700 in fines and car impoundment fees—but then, in the vast majority of cases, charges are dropped. Male pimps are likewise rarely arrested.

Along with this sexism, racism also plays in the challenges and threats faced by prostitutes. ICASA says that while 40 percent of street prostitutes are women of color, women of color constitute 55 percent of those arrested and 85 percent of those sentenced to jail time.

Dealing with sexual abuse and related traumas is key to breaking the cycle of incarceration and abuse. But most prisons and jails offer little in the way of support groups and counseling, and it can be even harder to access free resources once women get out.

Piecing Together a Life

In Chicago, several former prostitutes report that they were finally able to leave the lifestyle after finding support groups and programs that addressed both substance abuse and the physical and psychological issues involved in their early lives. Many women have had success at Genesis House, the only institution in the city accredited by the courts as an alternative to jail time. Genesis House is a strict yearlong residential program available free to walk-ins and women referred by the courts.

"They're very gentle and patient with me and don't rush me into anything," says a thirty-two-year-old Genesis House resident who asked that her name not be used. "They're helping me build up all those things that had been ripped out of me by prostitution."

In general, recovering prostitutes and service providers have a tricky balance to keep. They need to avoid stigmatizing or condemning prostitution as a lifestyle choice and female sexuality as a whole while still acknowledging that, for many, prostitution is a piece of a painful puzzle they want to leave behind.

To break the cycle of sexual abuse, prostitution, drugs and incarceration, many women note that there must be fundamental change in a society that allows or even encourages the exploitation of children and women.

"If it wasn't for men you wouldn't have prostitution," Myers says. "They think it's a joke, she's having a ball. No she isn't! They think they didn't do anything wrong. Women need to be taught that their body isn't an offering or a sacrifice."

7

Male Orphans and Runaways Sometimes Turn to Prostitution

Eric P. Martin and Nikola Brabenec

Eric P. Martin and Nikola Brabenec write for Radio Prague, which broadcasts news and events concerning the Czech Republic.

A majority of the male prostitutes in Prague, Czech Republic, are orphans and runaways, some as young as eleven years old. Having no job skills, these boys turn to prostitution to survive. While most boys see prostitution as a temporary solution, they often continue to work as prostitutes because they become caught in a cycle of drug addiction. Unfortunately, many contract deadly sexually transmitted diseases.

Although at twenty-eight, Kevin is a former male prostitute, he comes here to meet up with friends who are still in the business. He says he hates the place, because it reminds him of the experiences he's had here. He had so many clients that he turned to the drug pervitin to stay awake all night.

"Here you meet bank officials, people in high positions and people with average jobs. And you meet them without thinking about it, because if you were to remember each client you had or didn't have then you would go crazy. But the people usually remember you, and that's the worst."

Kevin and two other former male prostitutes told Radio Prague what it's like for these children and young men who are one of Prague's human tourist attractions. They paint a bleak picture of predominantly orphans and runaways caught up in a world of drug addiction, isolation and the ever-present threat of sexually transmitted diseases [STDs].

They also say that many of these prostitutes begin when they're still children. And even though these three men have left the business, their future does not seem bright. All of the former prostitutes asked that we not use their last names.

Kevin's Story

Kevin began prostitution at sixteen while still in school. His first client was a family member of his teacher.

He quit three years ago because he couldn't get enough clients. He looked too old to compete with the more sought-after teenagers. And since he is Roma, he says prospective clients feared him because of negative Gypsy stereotypes. They thought he intended to rob them.

Laszlo Sumegh says more than two-thirds of the around eighty male prostitutes that come through his doors lived in orphanages. Another 7 percent were runaway children.

Like many of these prostitutes, Kevin was raised in an orphanage. The Czech Republic has more children in orphanages than any other E.U. [European Union] country. Kevin says when he left the Moravian children's home, he was unprepared for life.

"Nowadays, orphanages are not obligated to prepare their students for life by securing them a job, money or a place to live. So I ended up on the street because I was eighteen and had just gotten out of an orphanage."

Kevin says a café in the train station is where some prostitutes meet prospective clients. Except for the sounds of the station below and the freeway outside, the scene is like that of any other coffee house. That's until you've spent a few hours here. You may see young men and boys spend their time moving from table to table, sometimes being joined by older men, sometimes walking off with one of them.

"The client comes, walks around, sees someone he likes and takes a seat at the table. And it looks like they're just chatting, but usually the conversation goes like this: 'Where are you from? How much do you go for? What do you want to do?' And then you leave together."

Petr [a male prostitute] said he was in an[d] out of the orphanages during his childhood.

Helping Male Prostitutes

At Project Opportunity, an organization that helps these prostitutes, coordinator Laszlo Sumegh says more than two-thirds of the around eighty male prostitutes that come through his doors lived in orphanages. Another 7 percent were runaway children.

Mr. Sumegh, a painter who founded the organization, says he hates the term "rent boys." He says it's more accurate to use the somewhat-awkward term *"commercially sexually exploited children and young people."*

One of his organization's main goals is prevention and testing of sexually transmitted diseases. Because of a shortage of saliva tests, it has been unable to test for HIV for about a year, but the prevalence among its clients of other STDs is high.

"A little while ago, ten clients were tested voluntarily. Of those, eight tested positive for Hepatitis B and C. So preventive work is really important for the work we do with these young people."

Petr's Story

One such test revealed that then-prostitute Petr had both Hepatitis B and C. That's when the twenty-three-year-old quit prostitution. The sexually-transmitted liver disease is deadly if not treated.

Petr said he was in an out of the orphanages during his childhood. He started prostitution soon after he turned eighteen. He kept working in the business because he was hooked on pervitin, a highly addictive form of methamphetamine.

"From my point of view, it's awful. If I didn't have to do it, I wouldn't have done it. But I was forced to so I could pay for my dose. When I was still taking drugs, I was taking pervitin. I tried heroin about twice, I smoked pot, I drank. Everything you could consume I did."

Stepan [a male prostitute] says he began prostitution at sixteen when he ran away from his parents' home.

Petr started late compared to the other male prostitutes. Mr. Sumegh says the average age at Project Opportunity is seventeen. The prostitutes there say some boys start as young as eleven.

The UN children's agency UNICEF does not know exactly how many underage boys there are working in Prague, but Czech director Pavla Gomba says she has personally seen that child prostitution occurs here.

"It's quite probable that the type of prostitution in Prague is mostly homosexual, meaning young boys—some quite young, twelve or thirteen years old—that offer themselves or are being offered to be prostituted."

Ms. Gomba says a UNICEF-sponsored study expected to come out later this month [November 2004] will have a clearer picture of the city's child prostitution.

But why do children get involved in prostitution? One reason is probably the money, but these former prostitutes say that's a fleeting benefit.

Stepan's Story

Stepan says he began prostitution at sixteen when he ran away from his parents' home. He says he started because he could have sex and get paid for it. But when he turned eighteen, prostitution became a way to supplement the government money he received for his diabetes. He says it wasn't enough to live on. Now thirty-six, he continued prostitution for about fourteen years.

"At first a person doesn't realize what can happen. You start to realize it later, but you are so entrenched you don't really ask why you're doing it or how you're doing it. The main thing is that you are making some money to live off, but it's not like you have money to throw around. There are only a few well-off clients, and mostly only at the beginning. It is enough to survive, but not enough to live."

The men we talked to say new prostitutes are more popular for clients, so the earnings drop off over time. Stepan says the change in the prices they can charge fall dramatically.

"When a person starts, they make thousands of crowns. And when you're leaving the business, you end up with mini sub sandwiches or mini pizzas—for sex."

Project Opportunity's Laszlo Sumegh says business for these young male prostitutes is also seasonal. Male tourists are the most lucrative clients. Many of the prostitutes are homeless, and tourists often hire them to stay in their hotel rooms for a few days. But the tourists are not around all year.

"In the summer there are more tourists and fewer locals. In the winter there are only the local men, and hunger and misery grow among the forgotten children who live on the edge of society in the streets."

Leaving the Business

All three former prostitutes say it takes only will power to leave the business. But then what?

Petr speaks proudly of his new apartment, because until now he's had trouble finding stable living conditions. He hopes to look for a job once he has gone through more treatment for his hepatitis, but he is unsure what his new profession will be.

"Now I am going to government offices, because I just had an operation and I'm on sick leave. And what sort of work will I have in the future? I don't know yet. It depends what the government agencies offer me."

Stepan is receiv[ing] retirement benefits because his diabetes is advanced. He says he was not watching his diet when he was a prostitute.

But soon after he quit the business, he found work when he restored the ties with his family.

"It was not hard to stop at the point where I got back together with my family. They started supporting me, and I could get work in another profession. It was not hard to stop. You can stop doing it overnight."

Kevin works as a laborer in the construction industry, but he says there are times when his past makes it hard to find work.

"I experience this very unpleasant feeling when I go to a company and there is someone sitting there who was my client. I am asking this person for work, but he tells me there are no openings and he won't take me. That's really depressing for me, but it's really the simplest and easiest way for him to deal with it."

But back at the main train station, the boys and young men who work in Prague's sex tourism industry are bracing for another cold winter, the time when work is scarce.

8

Sexual Liberation Has Led to the Toleration of Prostitution

Roger Scruton

Roger Scruton is a British writer and political activist.

Society's refusal to distinguish between moral and immoral sexual behavior has led to the toleration of prostitution. In a culture where girls are encouraged to be as promiscuous as boys and where marriage is reduced to a financial transaction, it is no surprise that prostitution has become accepted. Unfortunately, those who condone prostitution do not have to deal with the horrors experienced by its victims, often women and children who are sold into sexual servitude.

As part of hosting the World Cup [held in late June and early July 2006], the German government is preparing to ship in prostitutes for the use of the spectators, building special huts around the stadium, and—it seems—not asking too many questions about who obtains the women, by what method, and from where. This is one small but significant instance of a shift in attitude that has recently occurred in Europe. The oldest profession, which has survived for millennia without the benefit of public approval, is now officially endorsed—not merely legalized, but welcomed into the fold of the "inclusive society." It is even politically incorrect to use the term "prostitute": People on the left prefer "sex worker," implying that the hint of disapproval contained in the old name is a mark of discrimination that has no place in a postmodern society. Proposals to introduce trade-union rights and pension funds for these newly discovered "workers" have been debated in France and Germany, and the implication—that the state should tax their earnings—is accepted as entirely unproblematic. Visitors to Amsterdam have long been familiar with the market in female flesh that surrounds the Old Church. This church, the oldest in Amsterdam, is a symbol of Calvinist piety and famous for its music. On their way to the lesser business of worship, the choirboys now pass a window display of nudes, performing like sluggish snakes in their heated cages of glass. And, although the Dutch themselves have awoken, somewhat late, to the consequences of a demoralized public culture, the rest of Europe is intent on following their example, and sanitizing this last dark corner where the puritan conscience reigns.

Living with the Consequences

Official toleration is, in this matter as in so many others, the work of people largely protected from its consequences. Our legislators do not live in the areas of cities where prostitution is flagrant; they do not have to deal, in their daily lives, with the network of pimps and racketeers who live from the earnings of their female slaves; they do not have to fear for their daughters, now that the trade can be constantly resupplied from those places in the European hinterland where crime and cruelty are the norm. At the same time, so horrendous are the facts that the liberal conscience has an added reason for ignoring them. It is never pleasant, after all, to deal with the real consequences of human freedom. Prostitution in London, which was once a local industry among "fallen" women, supporting another local industry of philanthropists intent on rescuing them, is now largely run by illegal immigrants from the Balkans. These people do not conform to the standards adopted by the liberal conscience. The girls whom they bring with them are captured or purchased when too young to resist. Attempts to escape are severely punished by beating or torture, and communication with the outside world is expressly forbidden. Only in one particular do these girls conform to the ideal of the "sex worker" as now defined: Their earnings are taxed. That is to say, the pimp takes the lot, handing back what is required, as Marx would put it, "to reproduce their labor power." If ever there were a case of exploitation, this is it.

In a culture in which girls are encouraged to be as promiscuous as boys, it is hard to insist on an absolute distinction between the upright and the fallen woman.

It is still a crime in English law to "live off immoral earnings," though it is anyone's guess how long this provision will remain, now that the word "immoral," used in the vicinity of sex, is regarded as anachronistic. In any case, it is hard to punish this crime and harder still to prevent it. Witnesses are reluctant to come forward to accuse those members of the Albanian mafia who dominate the London scene; the girls themselves—often monoglot captives from the mountain villages—risk death should they make contact with the police. The customers are happy with a deal that offers youthful flesh at rock-bottom prices. And attempts to deport illegal immigrants are now more or less futile, with "human rights" lawyers specializing in offering Her Majesty's protection to Her Majesty's enemies. The idea that a modern Gladstone could walk the streets of Soho in order to rescue the victims of this trade is laughable. Even supposing there were such a person, able to survive the public mockery of his beliefs, he would not last long in a world where assassination is the normal way with intruders.

The Upright and the Fallen

Many factors have contributed to our current demoralization. Perhaps the most important is that to which I have already referred: the refusal to believe that there are "immoral earnings." In a culture in which girls are encouraged to be as promiscuous as boys, it is hard to insist on an absolute distinction between the upright and the fallen woman. Sexual liberation has made disapproval into a private matter, to be expressly kept out of the public domain. And women themselves have every reason to sympathize with the prostitute. Many of them, encouraged along the path of liberation, discover that sex really does have a cost. The men come and go, leaving heartbreak and insecurity in their wake. And if sex has a cost, why not insist on compensation? A woman who gives herself begins to look like a fool, when she gives herself for nothing. Why not sell herself instead? At least she will stand a chance of a fair and honest deal.

The prostitute used to be seen as the enemy of respectable women. She threatened the bargaining power of her sex, by offering cheaply what others were trying to offer at the highest possible price, namely marriage. She was immoral not because she satisfied the masculine urge to sow wild oats, but because she compromised the status of women, as companions who could not be purchased for an hour, but only for a lifetime. Sexual liberation has rubbed out that clear perception of the matter. Even if many people still feel that there is something sordid in reducing sex to a financial transaction, the difference between prostitution and marriage, in a world of prenuptial contracts and no-fault divorce, is, in the eyes of many people, no more than a difference of degree. Prostitution no longer looks like a threat to the moral order: At worst it is a threat to the woman, who puts herself at the mercy of strangers while at the same time removing any motive they might have to respect her.

Degrading Ideal Beauty

But there is more to the matter than that implies. For instance, there is the problem posed by beauty. Female beauty is a powerful social force—more powerful than money, more powerful than physical strength or intellectual acumen. The Trojans were destroyed by the beauty of Helen, Dante redeemed by the beauty of Beatrice, postwar Britain restored by the beauty of the young Queen Elizabeth. Hence we are in awe of female beauty and reluctant to see it as a physical asset, or to allow it to be marketed for its financial worth. Beauty is a symbol of the ideal. It cannot be possessed or consumed, any more than a melody in music can be possessed or consumed by the listener. It is forever unassimilable, a mark of the inherent meaning and purposefulness of human life. In the presence of beauty, therefore, we are inclined to adore, to worship, to sacrifice. For this reason beauty is a powerful stimulus to marriage, and beautiful women who marry do a lasting service to their sex. They cease to be competitors, and at the same time set an example. All women can take hope from them, knowing that, in the light that shines from a face that is both beautiful and devoted, they too may exhibit some reflected glow.

But suppose a beautiful woman takes the other path. There is no limit to the amount of money that a Brigitte Bardot or a Marilyn Monroe could command as a whore, no limit to the havoc she could create on the rare occasions when she would be compelled by financial necessity to cash in her assets. And by behaving in this way she would also degrade the idea of beauty: No woman could easily be set on a pedestal in a world where the fiscal benefits of beauty are fully exploited. And it would be a world full of anger, a world as threatened as Troy was threatened, once Helen was brought within its walls.

Aristocratic societies have solved the problem of beauty through the institution of the courtesan, whose presence helps to reconcile the otherwise conflicting conditions of sociable leisure and faithful marriage. The courtesan is not a prostitute, and cannot be purchased by money alone. She must be courted and flirted with; she must be lured into a quasi marriage, in which she enjoys protection for a finite time while retaining her independence and her social freedom. Her role depends on her beauty, whose destructive potential is neutralized by her temporary attachments. She protects chaste women from predators, to whom she is easy game. And she offers mild temptation to husbands, thereby peppering the bland diet of marriage with the spice of jealousy. Outside the peculiar conditions of an aristocratic culture, however, the courtesan cannot survive. She is the first casualty of sexual liberation. By placing aristocratic freedoms within the reach of every attractive woman, liberation deprives those freedoms of their glamour and therefore of their point.

This cold, hard meeting of strangers [prostitute and client] in total intimacy constitutes a deep violation of intimacy and all that it means.

The Body As Possession

Prostitution of the kind that we now witness in Europe, in which children are captured or sold into servitude, is hardly a crime on the victim's part. She cannot be blamed for a career into which she is forced by violence and intimidation, and from which she can escape only by risking her life. But her condition shows what is wrong with her trade. The one who volunteers for that trade is treating herself exactly as the pimp treats his victim. She is acting at one remove from her body, which has become a thing to be exploited, rather than the thing that she is.

The human body is not a possession; it is—to use the theological term—an incarnation. It is a subject, the focus and source of personal love, and not a mere object to be used. A woman doesn't own her body, any more than she owns herself. She is inextricably mingled with it, and what is done to her body is done to her. If she sells her body for sex, it is not sex that she is selling. For sex can be sincerely offered only if it is sincerely wanted by the one who offers it. Both prostitute and client are therefore engaged in an elaborate deception, each cheating the other, the one by pretending to sell sex, the other by pretending to buy it. Sex and contempt are adjacent regions in the psyche of the typical client; and a prostitute must willingly accept that she is being spat upon. The transaction that unites her to her partner also divides them, and this cold, hard meeting of strangers in total intimacy constitutes a deep violation of intimacy and all that it means.

It is odd that the German government should be offering this public endorsement to prostitution, at a time when that government is led by a woman. For women are acutely aware of the nature of sex, as a tribute from one self to another. To treat it as a commodity that can be bought and sold is not to offer it but to destroy it. The condemnation of prostitution was not just puritan bigotry; it was a recognition of a profound truth, which is that you and your body are not two things but one, and by abusing the body you harden the soul. Women have always been aware of that, and as a result have both feared prostitution and also been tempted by it, since it is a road out of womanhood and an escape from the burdens of womanly love. However it is a road that is seldom traveled in the opposite direction.

9

Gender-Based Domination Promotes Prostitution and Sex Trafficking

Monica O'Connor and Grainne Healy

Monica O'Connor is an activist and coauthor of publications on violence against women. Grainne Healy is a feminist activist and Chairwoman of the European Women's Lobby's Observatory on Violence Against Women.

Prostitution is male violence against women, a tool used by men worldwide to oppress women and children. Promoting the legalization of prostitution fosters the idea that men have the right to buy women to satisfy men's sexual needs. Legalization therefore thwarts efforts to promote gender equality and excludes sexually exploited women and children from laws that protect human rights. Gender equality can only be achieved when men are no longer allowed to buy and sell women and children.

Gender inequality is inherent in the promotion and normalisation of prostitution. Enshrined within state legislation, men's right to buy women is a direct contradiction to a society based on gender equality.

Promoting the idea that some women must be available for sale to satisfy men's sexual needs is to create a group of women who are excluded from the protection afforded under national and international human rights law.

Monica O'Connor and Grainne Healy, "Social/Gender Equality Consequences of Trafficking and Prostitution," *The Links Between Prostitution and Sex Trafficking: A Briefing Handbook.* CATW-EWL 2006. Reproduced by permission.

Prostitution and trafficking promotes sexism and racism as men are encouraged to see women from poorer foreign countries as less, as "other" and as legitimate targets for exploitation.

The Dangers of Legitimisation

It is not acceptable for states that call themselves democratic to legalise men's sexual exploitation of women. By legalising brothels and other prostitution related activities, these states are saying that it is right that women, and in some cases children, can and will be put up for sale, bought and consumed like any other commodity.

Legitimising prostitution will thwart efforts towards reciprocal, equal, just and empowering relationships between women and men and will retard the development of humane communities. More boys and men will be socialized to maltreat women as normal practice, thus progressively also dehumanising men. More girls and women will be drawn into prostitution, violated, and the individual and collective rights of women will be eroded.

The Swedish Government has long given priority to combating prostitution and trafficking in human beings for sexual purposes. This objective is an important part of Sweden's goal for equality between women and men, at the national level as well as internationally. Gender equality will remain unattainable as long as men buy, sell and exploit women and children by prostituting them.

Where feminists seek to transform sexuality in the interests of keeping women and children safe and ending women's inequality, the libertarians seek to promote and legitimise the traditional sexuality of dominance and submission. They eroticise practices that rely on power imbalance, such as sadomasochism, butch and femme, and so-called erotica that display women's humiliation and degradation. They see themselves as being in the so-called prosex tradition. Prosex turns out to mean prosexual dominance and submission.

The Consequences of Trafficking and Prostitution

Respect for women's bodies, and this respect's significance for our understanding of what it means to be a woman or a man and which rights that ensue, are totally dependent on if women are to be available for purchase.

We cannot dissociate prostitution from other forms of male violence against women and girls; nor from the systematic subordination by males of females in all countries around the world. In a patriarchy, male violence against women is one of the most powerful tools used to keep women and girls in a state of oppression and slavery.

Sexual exploitation preys on women and children made vulnerable by poverty and economic development policies and practices, refugee and displaced persons and on women in the migrating process. Sexual exploitation eroticises women's inequality and is a vehicle for racism and "first world" domination, disproportionately victimizing minority and "third world" women.

Currently the Internet is being used by men to promote and engage in the sexual exploitation of women... Men describe, often in graphic detail, their experience of using women and children. The women are completely objectified and evaluated on everything from skin colour to presence of scars and firmness of flesh. The men buying women and posting the information on the Internet see and perceive the events only from their self-interested perspective. Their awareness of racism, colonization, global economic inequalities and of course sexism is limited to how those forces affect them. A country's economic or political crisis and the accompanying poverty are advantages, which produce cheap labour for men. Often men describe how desperate the women are and how little men have to pay.

10

Drug Addiction Keeps Sex-Trafficking Victims in Prostitution

Nicholas D. Kristof

Nicholas D. Kristof is an editorial columnist for the New York Times.

Many teen prostitutes who have been liberated from Southeast Asian brothels return to the brothel because they are addicted to drugs. In fact, many brothel owners believe that addiction will keep prostitutes dependent on them. The girls trafficked into prostitution are also so broken and ashamed that the brothel is the only place where they have any self-esteem. The best way to reduce prostitution is therefore to prevent the trafficking of women and girls in the first place.

After I purchased Srey Mom from her brothel for $203 [in 2004] and brought her back to her village, the joy was overwhelming. Her parents and siblings had assumed she was dead, and they shrieked and hugged and cried.

I had doubts about the other sex slave I had purchased, Srey Neth, . . . who in fact is thriving and is now preparing to become a hairdresser. But I was pretty sure that Srey Mom would make it.

So I'm devastated to say that a year later [in 2005], I found Srey Mom back here in the wild town of Poipet, in her old brothel. She's devastated, too—when she spotted me, she ran away to her room in the back of the brothel until she could compose herself.

"I never lie to people, but I lied to you," she said forlornly. "I said I would not come back, and I did. I didn't want to return, but I did."

Yet, sadly, such an experience is common. Aid groups find it unnerving that they liberate teenagers from the bleak back rooms of a brothel, take them to a nice shelter—and then at night the kids sometimes climb over the walls and run back to the brothel.

It would be a tidier world if slaves always sought freedom. But prostitutes often are shattered and stigmatized, and sometimes they feel that the only place they can hold their head high is in the brothel.

Some brothel owners welcome addiction, because it makes the girls dependent upon them.

Srey Mom, too, has zero self-esteem, but in her case no one in her village knew her background, and she was clear of debts. The central problem, as best I can piece together the situation, is that she was addicted to methamphetamines, and that craving destroyed her will power, sending her fleeing back to the brothel so that she could get her drugs. . . .

An aid group looking after Srey Mom, American Assistance for Cambodia, gave her several more chances, once bringing her to Phnom Penh to enroll in school to become a hairdresser. But each time, Srey Mom fled back to drugs and the brothel.

"Ninety-five percent of the girls take drugs," Srey Mom told me. Some girls inject morphine, but brothel owners worry that needle holes make girls look unsightly, so methamphetamine pills are most common.

Some brothel owners welcome addiction, because it makes the girls dependent upon them. But Srey Mom said that is not true of her brothel owner, Heok Tem, whom she calls "Mother."

"Mother doesn't want us to use drugs," Srey Mom said. She has an eerily close relationship with Mrs. Heok Tem, and these days that emotional bond keeps her in the brothel as much as do her debts. Mrs. Heok Tem seems to feel genuine affection for Srey Mom and truly helped in the effort to get Srey Mom to start a new life, but she also cheats Srey Mom ruthlessly—I examined the brothel's account books—and rakes in cash by pimping the girl, which exposes her to AIDS.

"It's wrong," Mrs. Heok Tem admitted. But for now, she says, she needs the money.

Srey Mom still says her dream is to start life over in her village. "I want to go away," she said. "I don't want to stay here long. I'm not happy here. I will just look after my younger sisters. I'm already bad, and I don't want them to become bad like me."

I don't believe it will ever happen. I hate to write anyone off, but I'm afraid that Srey Mom will remain in the brothel until she is dying of AIDS (36 percent of girls in local brothels have HIV, and eventually it catches up with almost all of them). I finally dared tell her my fear. I described some young women I had just seen, gaunt and groaning, dying of AIDS in Poipet, and I told her I feared she would end up the same way.

"I'm afraid of that, too," she replied, her voice breaking. "This is an unhappy life. I don't want to do this."

Maybe that's what I find saddest about Srey Mom: She is a wonderful, good-hearted girl who gives money to beggars, who offers Buddhist prayers for redemption—but who is already so broken that she seems unable to escape a world that she hates and knows is killing her.

President [George W.] Bush declared in his [2005] inaugural address this week that "no one deserves to be a slave" and that advancing freedom is "the calling of our time." I can't think of a better place to start than the hundreds of thousands of girls trafficked each year, for this twenty-first-century version of slavery has not only grown in recent years but is also especially diabolical—it poisons its victims, like Srey Mom, so that eventually chains are often redundant.

11

Ignorance and Complacency Promote Sex Trafficking

Wendy Murray Zoba

Wendy Murray Zoba, the wife of an evangelical pastor and author of four books, writes for Christianity Today.

Sex trafficking is a serious problem that continues to grow due to ignorance and complacency. Some do not see sex trafficking as a serious problem because they believe that prostitution is a natural phenomenon: "Boys will be boys." Others see prostitutes as women who enjoy sex for profit. However, no one chooses to be a prostitute. Prostitution does not empower women, it degrades them. As long as people believe that men have the right to buy women for sex, there will be a market for sex trafficking.

Sex trafficking is buying and selling human beings (usually women and children)—and recruiting, transporting, transferring, and harboring them—for sexual exploitation. It is illegal in most countries and violates the Universal Declaration of Human Rights (1948), which asserts that "everyone has the right to life, liberty, and security of person," and that "no one shall be held in slavery or servitude [or] ... be submitted to torture." It is a vastly misunderstood crime, because many people tend to perceive prostitutes as willing participants in a "trade." And some gatekeepers of public morality—such as corrupt local police—often fail to defend, let alone rescue, the victimized women and children. Trafficked people are thus twice discarded.

Wendy Murray Zoba, "The Hidden Slavery," *Christianity Today*, vol. 47, November 2003, p. 68. Copyright 2003 Christianity Today, Inc. Reproduced by permission.

Disposable People

Researchers estimate that two million people are enslaved by the international sex market (as opposed to the general slave labor market). Numbers in the U.S. domestic sex market reach the hundreds of thousands. "There are more slaves alive today than all the people stolen from Africa," notes Kevin Bales in his book *Disposable People* (Univ. of California Press, 2000).

Forces of modernization have accelerated the resurgence of this "new slavery," as Bales calls it. The dramatic increase in world population, tripling since 1945 (from about 2 to 6 billion), has overwhelmed some developing countries. Rampant unemployment and underemployment give rise to masses of desperate people, producing what Bales calls "a glut of potential slaves."

Providing a Supply

"Sending" countries supply women and children. Trafficking flourishes, notably, in regions with the greatest population growth: Southeast Asia, the Indian subcontinent, Africa and the Arab world. Rapid social and economic change has meant that poverty has worsened for the underclass while the gap between rich and poor has widened. Women and children in economically desperate situations easily fall prey to tricks of traffickers.

They are then moved to "transit" countries—Mexico and Canada, for example, where they can more easily slip illegally into "receiving" countries like the United States, though Mexico and Canada do their own share of sending and receiving respectively.

The United States, Germany, and Italy are the top three destination countries, with the Netherlands and Japan close behind. According to one report by the UN Office on Drugs and Crime (May 2003), receiving countries are typically developed nations.

An estimated 45,000 to 50,000 foreign women and children cross the U.S. borders each year as fodder for sex trafficking. A layer down, intrastate domestic trafficking networks trade 300,000 to a million each year, according to the Center for Missing and Exploited Children [CMEC]. (The fluid and secretive nature of the trade makes it hard to pin down more specific numbers, CMEC explains.) Domestically or internationally, the script is the same: desperate women are lured with false promises. In the United States, for example, they are promised work as an au pair or a secretary, a waitress or a maid. But when they arrive at their destinations, the jobs aren't there. They end up in massage parlors, escort services, and dance clubs. They are told they must pay the expenses incurred in finding a job: transportation, rent, food. But in order to earn their keep, the women and children are forced to sell their bodies—at least "temporarily," they are told. But their so-called expenses outpace their income, and victims find it almost impossible to buy themselves out of their captors' clutches.

The New Abolitionists

Sex trafficking is a sophisticated network that pays off sweetly. In *The Inner Voice of Love*, Henri Nouwen describes a "deep abyss" in every human heart. It is impossible to fill, he says, because the needs are inexhaustible. "You have to work around it so that gradually the abyss closes."

The so-called good old boy mentality . . . reduces the sex trade to a 'boys will be boys' proposition, which breeds complacency and a lack of political will.

It is similarly impossible to fill the abyss that is sex trafficking. The drives that fuel it—both greed and sexual desire—are insatiable, still, local champions have arisen. In concert, from various fronts and on differing levels here and abroad, they are working around the abyss. Four mentioned here represent only a few frontline activists among countless others.

The Salvation Army's sprightly but fierce Lisa Thompson, sharply bedecked in the Army's signature blue and brass, leads the church's Initiative Against Sexual Trafficking (www.iast.net), which works with over thirty ministries, social agencies, denominational groups, and mission organizations that attack the problem. Thompson and IAST members write letters to legislators and religious authorities, speak in churches, at conferences, and universities, and generally try to create trouble for those who feed or abet this scourge.

The so-called good old boy mentality is a formidable opponent, she says. It reduces the sex trade to a "boys will be boys" proposition, which breeds complacency and a lack of political will. Thompson is determined to change that.

A Lack of Political Will

"The historical approach has been to penalize the women as wanton creatures who love sex and want easy money," she says. "But prostitution is not about the women. It is buying and selling human flesh that enables men to have their stable of women for sex without consequences. If you're serious about stopping sex trafficking, then you've got to be serious about the sex industry in general and all its disgusting and multifarious forms. Lack of political will in communities blinds them to what is going on in the 'gentlemen's club' on the corner. It is a blight on communities and the breeding ground for other criminal activity. It is time for law enforcement, prosecutors, and churches to spend time and resources to combat it."

Many U.S. laws need to be changed. In some states, it's merely a misdemeanor to pimp, a slap on the wrist for people who are essentially traffickers. The most powerful element in the demand-supply-distribution network, pimps are too often back on the streets after paying a fine or spending a night or two behind bars.

Thompson also says she hopes to fight bad laws before they're instituted. Among them is a proposal in Nevada to tax the proceeds from prostitution. "This would be a disaster," she says. "Once the lawmakers see prostitution as a solution to their budget problems, we'll have prostitution all over the place."

Battling Complacency

Self-described feminist Donna Hughes, a professor of women's studies at the University of Rhode Island, combats complacency in the academy. Through articles in academic journals, television appearances, and op-eds she rallies Christians and women's groups to unite in this moral battle.

What motivates her to fight, Hughes says, is the global movement to legalize prostitution, to "clean it up." Prostitution, so goes this line of thought, "empowers" the women who "choose" the vocation. Prostitution is already legal in the Netherlands, Germany, and Australia, and many other nations are considering whether to follow suit. Advocates argue that even prostitutes can possess dignity, but Hughes counters that dignity cannot arise from an industry that misuses and molests women.

'If you don't understand this issue, you're probably buying the lie that prostitution is a choice.'

She believes that "cleaning up" prostitution and removing legal constraints actually propels the sex-trafficking industry. The Netherlands is a case in point. The sex industry there is a billion-dollar business that accounts for 5 percent of the economy, an increase of 25 percent in ten years. Women in the industry come from thirty-two different countries, signaling a "predatory dependence on foreign women to meet the demand for flesh in Dutch brothels," to quote from a letter to Pope John Paul II, which Hughes signed. The government has a vested interest "in maintaining the transnational flow of women and children for commercial sexual exploitation" because the financial stakes are so high.

Unwittingly Promoting Trafficking

Hughes commends the [U.S.] State Department's Laura Lederer for breaking new ground in foreign aid policies. Some government aid agencies, in an attempt to "minimize harm" to those active in the sex trade, have unwittingly acquiesced to the trend of normalizing this behavior. Lederer, a senior adviser on trafficking in the Office of Global Affairs at the U.S. Department of State, has waged this "epic battle" (her words) at the highest levels of government for over ten years. She describes one telling incident from a conference on child trafficking at the Columbia School of Public Health in New York. "A wonderful group of doctors, nurses, public health officials and NGOs [non-governmental organization] presented their work from all around the world. One NGO gave a slide presentation that showed a small building behind a medical clinic. It turned out that children—six, seven, and eight years old— were coming [for treatment] because they were involved in what the NGO called 'sex work.' The slide presentation highlighted [workers] teaching young women and children how to use condoms and how to say in English, Japanese, and German, 'Please use a condom when you penetrate me.' What started out as a way to keep young women and children from getting and spreading AIDS had become part of the sex industry. Nobody was saying, 'This is illegal everywhere around the world, and we need to intervene.' They were making it possible for men to have access to younger and younger children." . . .

President Bush issued a National Security Presidential Directive (NSPD) in February [2003] that called prostitution inherently harmful and degrading to women and stressed the importance of identifying, protecting, and assisting victims exploited by traffickers. It was the first NSPD ever issued on trafficking. The NSPD, in turn, prompted USAID [U.S. Agency for International Development] administrator Andrew S. Natsios to announce the agency's intention to fund only those NGOs that will "monitor and combat this horrendous attack on the fundamental rights of vulnerable populations." In other words, USAID has moved from a position of "minimizing harm" to one of "report and rescue." Exactly how aid workers on the ground are to go about the "reporting and rescuing," Lederer says, is messy and still being worked out.

"People object that they aren't able to discern who is being trafficked and fear that monitoring it will put people in danger," she says. She concedes that aid workers are not police officers. At the same time, they are not powerless. "Anybody who encounters a six- or seven-year-old in a brothel can be assured that child is trafficked. They need to report to embassies, making it clear they've seen something illegal."

Hidden in Plain Sight

Thompson, Hughes, and Lederer are working at the grassroots, academic, and national levels. Al Erickson, in the meantime, works in the church. A quiet, simple pastor in the Evangelical Lutheran Church in America, he has learned dearly what the sex trade can do to a family.

The reticence ... among Christians to face this issue ...
is due in large part to the lack of knowledge about how
sexual exploitation works.

In the late 1980s, a person whom he only describes as his "loved one" faced a hard time in college and found solace in the company of a polished young man she met at a Christian gathering. She eventually followed him to California—"which was a dumb thing to do, but people do dumb things," Erickson says—and ended up drugged and forced into prostitution at the point of semiautomatic weapons. "You're caught in a terrorizing world," he says. "If you don't understand this issue, you're probably buying the lie that prostitution is a choice and so think, 'My kid would never make that choice.' It is violent and ugly and needs to be exposed for what it really is."

Erickson is founder and director of Adults Saving Kids (www.adultssavingkids.org), a church-based ministry to help families protect their children. Erickson's denomination has issued "A Message on Commercial Sexual Exploitation," which explains sexual exploitation and what churches can do to combat it. The statement is a model other churches and denominations are following.

Erickson is troubled by the reticence he senses among Christians to face this issue honestly and boldly. It is due in large part to the lack of knowledge about how sexual exploitation works and what is at stake. Heidi, who knows Erickson and his work, concurs: "In every church there are husbands addicted to pornography, a child who may be being seduced, or a woman who was once trapped in prostitution. But they can't talk about it in church. So they keep it inside as a dark secret."

Donna Hughes says the sex trade "is hiding in plain sight, in massage parlors you pass in shopping centers, in escort services advertised in your Yellow Pages." She . . . and Thompson and Lederer and Erickson would join in chorus encouraging citizens to act.

12

Multiple Factors Contribute to Child Sex Tourism

Sowmia Nair

Sowmia Nair is an agent of the U.S. Department of Justice.

Child-sex tourists travel to foreign countries to have sex with children—a crime in their home country. One of the most significant factors that contributes to this horrific practice is poverty. Children, lured from home with the promise of jobs, are forced into prostitution. The Internet also encourages child sex tourism by supplying tourists with information on how to procure child prostitutes. In addition, foreign governments, hoping to improve economic conditions by promoting tourism, often turn a blind eye to its darker side.

> *"On this trip, I've had sex with a fourteen year-old girl in Mexico and a fifteen year-old in Colombia. I'm helping them financially. If they don't have sex with me, they may not have enough food. If someone has a problem with me doing this, let UNICEF [United Nation's Children's Fund] feed them."*
>
> *—Retired U.S. Schoolteacher*

The international tourism industry is booming. Since the 1960s, international travel has increased seven-fold. As tourists eagerly travel to distant lands to enjoy new landscapes and cultures, economically developing countries have welcomed the expansion of the international tourism industry as a much-needed source of income within their own nations. With the exponential rise in this industry, however, comes the growth of a darker, more clandestine phenomenon: child sex tourism.

Sowmia Nair, "Child Sex Tourism," U.S. Department of Justice: Child Exploitation and Obscenity Section.

A Lucrative Global Industry

Sex tourism is a very lucrative industry that spans the globe. In 1998, the International Labour Organization reported its calculations that 2–14 percent of the gross domestic product of Indonesia, Malaysia, the Philippines, and Thailand derives from sex tourism. In addition, while Asian countries, including Thailand, India, and the Philippines, have long been prime destinations for child-sex tourists, in recent years, tourists have increasingly traveled to Mexico and Central America for their sexual exploits as well.

Actions by foreign governments may directly or indirectly encourage child-sex tourism.

Child-sex tourists are individuals that travel to foreign countries to engage in sexual activity with children. The nonprofit organization End Child Prostitution, Child Pornography, and the Trafficking of Children (ECPAT) estimates that more than one million children worldwide are drawn into the sex trade each year.

Factors Supporting the Child-Sex Trade

The most significant societal factor that pushes children into prostitution is poverty. Many nations with thriving sex tourism industries are nations that suffer from widespread poverty resulting from turbulent politics and unstable economies. Poverty often correlates with illiteracy, limited employment opportunities, and bleak financial circumstances for families. Children in these families become easy targets for procurement agents in search of young children. They are lured away from broken homes by "recruiters" who promise them jobs in a city and then force the children into prostitution. Some poor families themselves prostitute their children or sell their children into the sex trade to obtain desperately needed money. Gender discrimination also works in tandem with poverty; in many countries, female children have fewer educational opportunities or prospects for substantial employment. Consequently, they must find other means of earning a living.

The Internet has also facilitated the recent rise in child-sex tourism by providing a convenient marketing channel. Web sites provide potential child-sex tourists with pornographic accounts written by other child-sex tourists. These Web sites detail sexual exploits with children and supply information on sex establishments and prices in various destinations, including information on how to specifically procure child prostitutes. Additionally, sex-tour travel agents may publish brochures and guides on the Internet that cater to child-sex tourists. In 1995, there were over twenty-five businesses in the United States that offered and arranged sex tours. One particular Web site promised nights of sex "with two young Thai girls for the price of a tank of gas." The easy availability of this information on the Internet generates interest in child-sex tourism and facilitates child-sex abusers in making their travel plans.

Finally, actions by foreign governments may directly or indirectly encourage child-sex tourism. National governments in countries which are struggling economically have become increasingly tourist-oriented in their search for profitable sources of income. These governments sometimes turn a blind eye to the sex tourism industry, thus allowing the industry to perpetuate sexual exploitation upon children in order to encourage tourism in their country in general.

The Victims of Child-Sex Tourism

Child-sex tourism makes its profits from the exploitation of child prostitutes in developing countries. Many children are trafficked into the sex trade. In Thailand, for example, Burmese girls as young as thirteen are illegally trafficked across the border by recruiters and sold to brothel owners.

The lives of child prostitutes are almost too appalling to confront. Studies indicate that child prostitutes serve between two and thirty clients per week, leading to a shocking estimated base of anywhere between 100 to 1,500 clients per year, per child. Younger children, many below the age of ten, have been increasingly drawn into serving tourists.

Child prostitutes live in constant fear; they live in fear of sadistic acts by clients, fear of being beaten by pimps who control the sex trade, and fear of being apprehended by the police. It comes as no surprise that victims often suffer from depression, low self-esteem, and feelings of hopelessness.

Anonymity provides the child-sex tourist with freedom from the moral restraints that govern behavior in his home country.

Many victims of child sexual exploitation also suffer from physical ailments, including tuberculosis, exhaustion, infections, and physical injuries resulting from violence inflicted upon them. Venereal diseases run rampant among these children and they rarely receive medical treatment until they are seriously or terminally ill. Living conditions are poor and meals are inadequate and irregular. Many children that fail to earn enough money are punished severely, often through beatings and starvation. Sadly, drug use and suicide are all too common for victims of child sexual exploitation.

Child-Sex Tourists

Child-sex tourists are typically males and come from all income brackets. Perpetrators usually hail from nations in Western European nations and North America.

While some tourists are pedophiles that preferentially seek out children for sexual relationships, many child-sex tourists are "situational abusers." These are individuals who do not consistently seek out children as sexual partners, but who do occasionally engage in sexual acts with children when the opportunity presents itself.

The distorted and disheartening rationales for child-sex tourism are numerous. Some perpetrators rationalize their sexual encounters with children with the idea that they are helping the children financially better themselves and their families. Paying a child for his or her services allows a tourist to avoid guilt by convincing himself he is helping the child and the child's family to escape economic hardship. Others try to justify their behavior by believing that children in foreign countries are less "sexually inhibited" and by believing their destination country does not have the same social taboos against having sex with children. Still other perpetrators are drawn towards child sex while abroad because they enjoy the anonymity that comes with being in a foreign land. This anonymity provides the child-sex tourist with freedom from the moral restraints that govern behavior in his home country. Consequently, some tourists feel that they can discard their moral values when traveling and avoid accountability for their behavior and its consequences. Finally, some sex tourists are fueled by racism and view the welfare of children of third-world countries as unimportant.

The International Response to Child-Sex Tourism

The response of destination countries to the epidemic of child-sex tourism has been ineffective. Although many of these countries have passed legislation that criminalizes sexual exploitation of children, these laws often remain unenforced against tourists. Efforts to combat child-sexual exploitation often run into conflict with foreign governments' efforts to promote the international tourism industry. Police corruption is common. In Thailand and the Philippines, police have been known to guard brothels and even procure children for prostitution. Some police in destination countries directly exploit children themselves. Thus far, the international community has not been able to rely on destination countries to adequately protect the rights and well-being of child victims.

The United States has risen to take legislative action against the growing evils of child-sex tourism. In 1994, Congress established 18 U.S.C. § 2423(b), which is aimed towards prosecution of child-sex tourists. Section 2423(b) criminalizes traveling abroad for the purpose of engaging in illegal sexual activity with a minor. Currently, successful prosecution under § 2423(b) requires the government to prove that an alleged child-sex tourist from the United States formed the intent to engage in sexual activity with a child prior to meeting the child and initiating sexual contact. In other words, a defendant is only punishable under § 2423(b) if he has the intent, while traveling, to engage in sexual activity with minors. The federal government has successfully utilized § 2423(b) to target several child-sex tourists. Current proposals to eliminate the intent requirement may broaden the government's prosecutorial power by allowing the government to prosecute U.S. citizens who engage in sexual acts with children while abroad, regardless of when they formed the intent to do so.

Child-sex tourism grows at an alarming rate and inflicts devastating consequences on millions of children around the globe. As a global leader, the United States is committed to using its power to reform and eradicate child-sex tourism industry.

Organizations to Contact

The editors have compiled the following list of organizations concerned with the issues debated in this book. The descriptions are derived from materials provided by the organizations. All have publications or information available for interested readers. The list was compiled on the date of publication of the present volume; the information provided here may change. Be aware that many organizations take several weeks or longer to respond to inquiries, so allow as much time as possible.

Alan Guttmacher Institute
120 Wall St., 21st Fl., New York, NY   10005
(212) 248-1111 • fax: (212) 248-1952
e-mail: info@guttmacher.org
Web site: www.guttmacher.org

The institute works to protect and expand the reproductive choices of all women and men. It strives to ensure that people have access to the information and services they need to exercise their rights and responsibilities concerning sexual activity, reproduction, and family planning. The institute publishes the following bimonthly journals: *Perspectives on Sexual and Reproductive Health, International Family Planning Perspectives*, and the *Guttmacher Report on Public Policy*. Selected articles from these publications, including "Ominous Convergence: Sex Trafficking, Prostitution, and International Family Planning" and "Global Concern for Children's Rights: The World Congress Against Sexual Exploitation," are available on its Web site.

American Civil Liberties Union (ACLU)
125 Broad St., 18th Fl., New York, NY   10004-2400
(212) 549-2500
e-mail: aclu@aclu.org
Web site: www.aclu.org

The ACLU champions the human rights set forth in the U.S. Constitution. It works to protect the rights of all Americans and to promote equality for women, minorities, and the poor. The ACLU opposes the U.S. Agency for International Development requirement that public health organizations and other groups that receive funding under the AIDS Leadership Act must adopt a written policy "explicitly opposing prostitution and sex trafficking." The organization publishes a variety of handbooks, pamphlets, reports, and newsletters, including the quarterly *Civil Liberties* and the monthly *Civil Liberties Alert*. The article "Global AIDS Gag Holds Critical Funding Captive to Politics" is available on its Web site.

Captive Daughters
3500 Overland Ave., Suite 110-108
Los Angeles, CA   90034-5696
fax: (310) 815-9197
e-mail: mail@captivedaughters.org
Web site: www.captivedaughters.org

The mission of Captive Daughters is to end the sexual bondage of female adolescents and children. Its goal is to educate the public about the worldwide problem of sex trafficking and to promote policies and action to prevent it. Its Web site publishes an annotated bibliography of books and films and previously published articles, including "Sex Trafficking: The Real Immigration Problem."

Coalition Against Trafficking in Women (CATW)
PO Box 9338, N., Amherst, MA   01059
fax: (413) 367-9262
e-mail: info@catwinternational.org
Website: www.catwinternational.org

CATW is a nongovernmental organization that promotes women's human rights. It works internationally to combat sexual exploitation in all its forms, especially prostitution and trafficking in women and children. CATW publishes articles, reports, and speeches on issues related to sex trafficking, including "On the Battlefield of Women's Bodies: An Overview of the Harm of War to Women" and "The Case Against the Legalization of Prostitution," which are available on its Web site.

Concerned Women for America (CWA)
1015 15th St. NW, Suite 1100, Washington, DC   20005
(202) 488-7000 • fax: (202) 488-0806
e-mail: mail@cwfa.org
Web site: www.cwfa.org

CWA works to strengthen marriage and the traditional family according to Judeo-Christian moral standards. It opposes abortion, pornography, homosexuality, and the legalization or decriminalization of prostitution. The organization publishes numerous brochures and policy papers as well as *Family Voice*, a monthly newsmagazine. Selected articles opposing the legalization or decriminalization of prostitution such as "Trafficking of Women and Children" are available on its Web site.

Free the Slaves
1012 14th Street NW, Suite 600, Washington, DC   20005
(202) 638-1865 • fax: (202) 638-0599
e-mail: info@freetheslaves.net
Web site: www.freetheslaves.net

Free the Slaves dedicates itself to ending slavery worldwide. It partners with grassroots antislavery organizations and concerned businesses to eradicate slavery from product supply chains and to build a consumer movement that chooses slave-free goods. Free the Slaves also encourages governments to draft and enforce effective antislavery and antitrafficking laws. The organization publishes reports such as "International Trafficking in Women to the United States: A Contemporary Manifestation of Slavery and Organized Crime," which is available on its Web site.

Global Rights
1200 18th Street NW, Suite 602, Washington, DC   20036
(202) 822-4600 • fax: (202) 822-4606
Web site: www.globalrights.org

Global Rights is a human rights advocacy group that partners with local activists worldwide to challenge injustice. The organization opposes U.S. laws that require organizations receiving U.S. global HIV/AIDS and antitrafficking funds to adopt organization-wide positions opposing prostitution. Global Rights claims that such laws restrict the ability of local activists to prevent the spread of AIDS and to advocate for the health and human rights of women and men in prostitution. It publishes the quarterly magazine *VOICES* and news, reports, and analysis on trafficking. Articles such as "Slavery in Our Midst: The Human Toll of Trafficking" are available on its Web site.

Human Rights Watch
350 5th Ave., 34th Fl., New York, NY   10118-3299
(212) 290-4700
e-mail: hrwnyc@hrw.org
Web site: www.hrw.org

Founded in 1978, this nongovernmental organization conducts systematic investigations of human rights abuses in countries around the world, including sex trafficking. It publishes many books and reports on specific countries and issues as well as annual reports, recent selections of which are available on its Web site.

International Justice Mission (IJM)
PO Box 58147, Washington, DC   20037-8147
(703) 465-5495 • fax: (703) 465-5499
e-mail: contact@ijm.org
Web site: www.ijm.org

IJM is a human rights agency that rescues victims of violence, sexual exploitation, slavery, and oppression. Its goals include rescuing victims, bringing accountability under the law to perpetrators, preventing future abuses, and helping victims transition to new lives. IJM publishes articles, reports, and books, including *Terrify No More*, which documents IJM's raids in the Cambodian village of Svay Pak, where its workers rescued thirty-seven underage victims of sex trafficking, many of them under the age of ten. The book can be purchased on its Web site for a small donation.

International Sex Worker Foundation for Art, Culture, and Education (ISWFACE)
801 Cedros Ave. #7, Panorama City, CA   91402
(818) 892-2029
e-mail: iswface@iswface.org
Web site: www.iswface.org

ISWFACE is an organization run by current and retired sex workers. It serves as an educational resource center for information about and research on prostitution and sex work. Its goal is to foster, perpetuate, and preserve an appreciation of the art and culture created by and about sex workers. Other goals include educating the public about sex workers, their art, and their culture, providing economic alternatives and opportunities for creative, artistic sex workers, and offering accurate, timely information about sex work to health care and law enforcement organizations.

Polaris Project
PO Box 77892, Washington, DC   20013
(202) 547-7990 • fax: (202) 547-6654
e-mail: info@polarisproject.org
Web site: www.polarisproject.org

The Polaris Project is a multicultural grassroots organization combating human trafficking and modern-day slavery. Based in the United States and Japan, it brings together community members, survivors, and professionals to fight trafficking and slavery. The project's goals include empowering trafficking survivors and effecting long-term social change to end trafficking.

Prostitution Research and Education (PRE)
PO Box 16254, San Francisco, CA 94116-0254
e-mail: contact1@prostitutionresearch.com
Web site: www.prostitutionresearch.com

PRE is a nonprofit organization whose goal is to abolish the institution of prostitution. PRE also gives voice to those who are among the world's most disenfranchised groups: prostituted/trafficked women and children. Publications include articles and reports on the legal, social, and health implications of prostitution and sex trafficking, including "Prostitution: Where Racism and Sexism Intersect" and "Prostitution, Violence, and Post-Traumatic Stress Disorder," which are available on its Web site.

Shared Hope International
PO Box 65337, Vancouver, WA 98665
1-866-HER-LIFE
e-mail: savelives@sharedhope.org
Web site: www.sharedhope.org

Shared Hope International is a nonprofit organization that exists to rescue and restore women and children in crisis. It establishes places to which trafficked women and children can escape and receive health care, education, and job training. Shared Hope International works with locally led efforts to rescue trafficked women and children. It also identifies areas of victimization to increase public awareness and builds alliances to eradicate human trafficking. Fact sheets and the article "Tracing the History of Sex Trafficking" are available on its Web site.

Women's Commission on Refugee Women and Children
122 E. 42nd St., 12th Fl., New York, NY 10168-1289
(212) 551-3088 • fax: (212) 551-3180
e-mail: info@womenscommission.org
Web site: www.womenscommission.org

The commission offers solutions and provides technical assistance to ensure that refugee women, children, and adolescents are protected and have access to education, health services, and livelihood opportunities. It makes recommendations to U.S. and United Nations policymakers and nongovernmental organizations on ways to improve assistance to refugee women and children. Experts conduct field research and technical training in refugee camps and detention centers. On its Web site the commission publishes issues of its semiannual newsletter, *Women's Commission News*, reports, and articles, including "The Struggle Between Migration Control and Victim Protection: The UK Approach to Human Trafficking."

World Vision International
800 W. Chestnut Ave., Monrovia, CA   91016
(626) 303-8811
e-mail: newsvision@wvi.org
Web site: ww.wvi.org

Established in 1950, World Vision International is a Christian relief and development organization that works for the well-being of all people, especially children. Through emergency relief, education, health care, economic development, and promotion of justice, World Vision's goal is to help communities help themselves. It publishes the quarterly *Global Future* and many reports and articles, many of which are available on its Web site, including "Children's Work, Adult's Play: Child-Sex Tourism—The Problem in Cambodia."

Bibliography

Books

Paul R. Abramson, Steven D. Pinkerton, and Mark Huppin — *Sexual Rights in America: The Ninth Amendment and the Pursuit of Happiness.* New York: New York University Press, 2003.

Kevin Bales — *Disposable People: New Slavery in the Global Economy.* Berkeley, CA: University of California Press, 2004.

Karen Beeks and Delil Amir, eds. — *Trafficking and the Global Sex Industry.* Lanham, MD: Lexington, 2006.

Joanna Brewis and Stephen Linstead — *Sex Work and Women's Labor Around the World.* Bloomington, IN: Indiana University Press, 2004.

Belinda Brooks-Gordon — *The Price of Sex: Prostitution, Policy and Society.* Portland, OR: Willan, 2006

Michel Dorais — *Rent Boys: The World of Male Sex Workers.* Montreal, Quebec: McGill-Queen's University Press, 2005.

Barbara Ehrenreich and Arlie Russell Hochschild, eds. — *Global Woman: Nannies, Maids, and Sex Workers in the New Economy.* New York: Metropolitan, 2003.

Melissa Farley, ed. — *Prostitution, Trafficking, and Traumatic Stress.* Binghamton, NY: Haworth, 2003.

Geetanjali
Gangoli

International Approaches to Prostitution: Law and Policy in Europe and Asia. Bristol, UK: Policy Press, 2006.

Kelly Gorkoff and
Jane Runner, eds.

Being Heard: The Experiences of Young Women in Prostitution. Black Point, Nova Scotia: Fernwood, 2003.

Kamala
Kempadoo, ed.

Trafficking and Prostitution Reconsidered: New Perspectives on Migration, Sex Work, and Human Rights. Boulder, CO: Paradigm, 2005.

Gilbert King

Woman, Child for Sale: The New Slave Trade in the 21st Century. New York: Chamberlain Bros., 2004.

Leonore Kuo

Prostitution Policy: Revolutionizing Practice Through a Gendered Perspective. New York: New York University Press, 2002.

Rachael Lindsay

Rachael: Woman of the Night. Cape Town, South Africa: Kwela, 2003.

Catharine A.
MacKinnon

Women's Lives, Men's Laws. Cambridge, MA: Belknap, 2005.

Victor Malarek

The Natashas: Inside the New Global Sex Trade. New York: Arcade, 2004.

Craig McGill

Human Traffic: Sex, Slaves, and Immigration. London, England: Vision, 2003.

Joyce Outshoorn, ed.	*The Politics of Prostitution: Women's Movements, Democratic States, and the Globalisation of Sex Commerce.* New York: Cambridge University Press, 2004.
Jody Raphael	*Listening to Olivia: Violence, Poverty, and Prostitution.* Boston: Northeastern University Press, 2004.
Teela Sanders	*Sex Work: A Risky Business.* Portland, OR: Willan, 2005.
Helen J. Self	*Prostitution, Women, and the Misuse of the Law: The Fallen Daughters of Eve.* Portland, OR: Frank Cass, 2003.
Siroj Sorajjakool	*Child Prostitution in Thailand: Listening to Rahab.* Binghamton, NY: Haworth, 2003.

Periodicals

Christina Ahn	"The Most Complicated Profession," *Women's Health Activist*, November–December 2004.
Libby Tata Arcel and Marianne C. Kastrup	"War, Women, and Health," *Nordic Journal of Women's Studies*, April 2004.
Brian Bergman	"Lost, Luckless Girls," *Maclean's*, May 23, 2005.
Bruce Bower	"Childhood's End," *Science News*, September 24, 2005.

Maddy Coy   "Leaving Care; Loathing Self," *Community Care*, February 3, 2005.

Matt Dougherty   "A Day in the Life of a Male Prostitute," *World Internet News*, December 2, 2005. http://soc.hfac.uh.edu.

Economist   "It's a Foreigner's Game," September 2, 2004.

Bay Fang   "Young Lives for Sale," *U.S. News & World Report*, October 24, 2005.

Amy Fraley   "Child-Sex Tourism Legislation Under the Protect Act: Does It Really Protect," *St. John's Law Review*, Spring 2005.

Barbara Gunnell   "Nothing to Sell but Their Bodies," *New Statesman*, March 1, 2004.

Harper's   "I Am Going to Burn," March 2004.

Angie Heal   "The Sex Trap," *Community Care*, June 10, 2004.

David Heinzmann   "Dark Path Starts at Early Age for Many Child Prostitutes," *Chicago Tribune*, August 7, 2005.

G. Derrick Hodge   "Sex Workers of Havana: The Lure of Things," *NACLA Report on the Americas*, January–February 2003.

Shu-ling Hwang   "Juveniles' Motivation for Remaining and Olwen   in Prostitution," *Psychology of Women Bedford   Quarterly*, June 2004.